Tim Sherwett

The Politics of Language

The Politics
of Language

Liberalism
as Word and
Symbol

Ronald D. Rotunda

Introduction by Daniel Schorr

Afterword by M. H. Hoeflich

University of Iowa Press
Iowa City

University of Iowa Press, Iowa City 52242

Copyright © 1986 by the University of Iowa

All rights reserved

Printed in the United States of America

First edition, 1986

Jacket and book design by Richard Hendel

Typesetting by G&S Typesetters, Inc., Austin, Texas

Printing and binding by Thomson-Shore, Inc., Dexter, Michigan

Library of Congress Cataloging-in-Publication Data

Rotunda, Ronald D.

    The politics of language.

    Includes index.

    1. Liberalism—United States—History. 2. Liberalism—Great Britain—
History. 3. Symbolism in politics. I. Title.

JA84.U5R69 1986   320.5′1   85-24548

ISBN 0-87745-139-7

TO BILL FREIVOGEL

*My lawyer, if I should
ever need one*

To "capture" a word such as democracy—that is, a word which has favorable emotive properties—is per se to assure oneself of a formidable position of strength. And to "surrender" to a word with negative associations—to accept for instance the term ideology as the proper label for all that we say in political matters—is in itself to start off with a handicap.

Giovanni Sartori,
Democratic Theory

Natural man, whether simpleton or scientist, knows no more of the linguistic forces that bear upon him than the savage knows of gravitational forces.

Benjamin Whorf,
Language, Thought, and Reality

Contents

Introduction
Daniel Schorr

In the aftermath of President Reagan's landslide reelection, I became involved in a spirited exchange of correspondence with a television viewer because I had allowed to go unchallenged a reference to the president as a "lame duck" by a participant in my program. The writer asked me to apologize for this unwarranted slur against a popular president. My explanation that "lame duck" was an unpejorative description of an officeholder who could not be reelected produced another angry letter citing a Webster dictionary definition of "lame duck" as an official serving out the remainder of a term after having been defeated. I was rescued by William Safire's *Political Dictionary*, a manual of "the new language of politics," providing a more current definition of "lame duck" as "an office-holder whose power is diminished because he is soon to leave office, as a result of defeat or *statutory limitation*" (italics very much mine).

This was an example of how the usage of words changes and how much passion can be generated by how they are used in politics. Indeed, words in politics are like emblems in wars and revolutions—to be flown, shot at, and sometimes captured. Word wars are not incidental but are central to political strife—especially as amplified in this era by the great megaphone of television.

As Democrats have appropriated the word "fair" (as in Fair Deal), so Republicans have laid siege to "free" (as in "free enterprise"). The word "new" is contested, the Democrats having produced the New Deal of FDR days and the Republicans counterattacking with New Federalism and, more recently, New Opportunity.

No word has been flown more proudly, disputed more hotly

and, finally, battered more decisively than "liberal." Its original association with the simple word "free" (Latin *liber*) became lost in antiquity as it became weighted with changing symbolism on its voyage through time and across the ocean from Europe. As might be expected, "liberal" carried a white-hat connotation during the long generations when liberals dominated the political scene. When the conservatives finally swept in from the wilderness and stormed the bastions of government, they swiftly attached black-hat connotations to the word. (My mail indicates that to call the news media "liberal" has become an accusation, needing no further detailed indictment.)

It is fascinating to look back on the vital role that liberalism has played in history. No single word, other than more general expressions like "rights," "freedom," and "justice," has played a more important role in America's political development. By telling us what has happened to a word, Ronald Rotunda has illuminated what has happened to America. It is done with meticulous regard for historical scholarship. Some day liberalism may make a comeback, but for now this book will serve as its epitaph.

The Politics of Language

1

Symbols in Politics and Law

Introduction

The ancients knew the importance of words. Genesis tells us that after the Lord "fashioned all the wild beasts and all the birds of heaven," the first order of priority was to bring them to Adam, "to see what he would call them; each one was to bear the name the man would give it. The man gave names to all the cattle, all the birds of heaven, and all the wild beasts." Naming things is important business.

This book is about naming things—about symbols and labels, the importance of words, their power to manipulate, and why people fight over them. In particular, it is a study of a specific word, "liberal."

The liberal label has been a very significant symbol in modern American political and legal history. And for most of this modern period, when we have spoken of liberal judges, the American liberal tradition, and liberal politicians, the adjective has had favorable connotations. In fact, the late Senator Robert Taft, as recently as 1950, argued that he was really liberal; he rejected the conservative tag in favor of the word that then had more favorable connotations.

In the 1980s liberalism seems to be in disarray, and many politicians who formerly embraced the liberal label now want to unpeel the tag. In 1964, when Barry Goldwater, an avowedly conservative Republican candidate, ran against a self-described liberal candidate, President Lyndon Johnson and his Great Society won a stunning victory. Yet only two decades later, the unabashedly conservative Ronald Reagan won an equally stunning reelection victory against the candidate of the liberals, Walter F. Mondale.

Much had changed in twenty years. Actually, more had changed than many people realize, for it is not generally remembered that "liberalism" is a relatively new term in American politics. The British liberals go back many years, but when the British Liberal party was in the ascendency in the early part of this century, there were no American politicians who called themselves liberal. Not until Franklin D. Roosevelt battled Herbert Hoover did the liberal label become important in the American lexicon; then both Hoover and Roosevelt claimed to be the true liberals, and the fight over the label dominated intellectual debate for much of the New Deal. Each politician sensed the favorable connotations of the word, and each tried to capture it. Roosevelt won, and since then the word has been used to describe such diverse groups as certain types of politicians, judges, and theologians.

The fascinating story of the rise and decline of the liberal label is not just a study in intellectual history; it is also a story of the importance of the use of symbols generally—how they reflect and mold the way we think and act. And it is the story of the limits on the power and use of symbols.

The Importance of Symbols

The "symbols of government"[1] are of fundamental importance in the study of politics and law. Perhaps because we have passed 1984 unscathed, we often ignore the significance of George Orwell's Newspeak. But governments know better. For example, in the large ancient governments— Alexander's empire, the Seleucids' monarchy, and the Roman empire—political, legal, and religious symbols generated loyalty. Sheldin Wolin has observed that "the use of symbolism was particularly important because it showed how valuable symbols can be in bridging vast distances. They serve to evoke the presence of authority despite the physical reality being far removed."[2] In the Middle Ages as well, leaders turned to symbols, sometimes ancient ones, to justify their rule.[3]

Symbols are still useful for generating loyalty in more modern governments. Professor Murray Edelman has astutely noted that "the most conspicuously democratic institutions are largely symbolic and expressive in function."[4] The English historian Walter Bagehot demonstrated how important the symbols of the monarch and the constitution are for the British. Justice Frankfurter recognized that the state must use symbols to inculcate indispensable feelings toward government because "symbolism is inescapable. Even the most sophisticated live by symbols."[5]

A symbol can carry great significance for an individual. That symbol becomes particularly significant whenever it has special meaning for a large number of people. Although there are those who belittle argument over mere words, one should realize that words are seldom innocuous, for they are our primary form of communication. Crucial concepts often lie in shades of meaning.

The disagreement in the late 1960s over the phrase "black power" was, in many respects, an argument over definition. In one Senate subcommittee hearing, for example, Senator Abraham Ribicoff warned Floyd McKissick, head of CORE and a black power advocate, "You make our job very hard when you put us up against such a slogan." McKissick replied that the slogan would not be changed. Senator Robert Kennedy then argued that "if people can't meet your definition, you read them out." McKissick retorted that he was not throwing anyone out of the movement and that he believed "black power" would be accepted just as "Irish power" had been accepted.[6] Two little words and what they represented split the civil-rights movement for a time, creating increased advocacy in some quarters and making new enemies out of former friends in others.

Symbols also enable leaders to give the *appearance* of action. It is very advantageous for leaders, especially in our democratic society, to be able at least to appear to be taking action. People like to think that something is being done about their problems; for short-range popularity it does not make much difference if something is actually done. Much of the history of antitrust legislation provides a beautiful example of the power of symbols to substitute for substance.

In 1890, under popular pressure, Congress passed a vague law against monopolies. The purpose of this Sherman Antitrust Act, a senator at that time said, was to pass "some bill headed: 'A bill to Punish Trusts' with which to go to the country."[7] Later, in 1914, Congress passed the Clayton Antitrust Act, hailed as "Labor's Magna Carta" by Samuel Gompers, since he thought the bill exempted labor from antitrust laws. In fact the Clayton Act, for much of its history, was used more effectively against labor than against capital.[8] Thurmond Arnold, in *The Folklore of Capitalism*, saw very clearly that symbolic legislation against the trusts convinced the average citizen that action had been taken. It did not matter that for the first forty years of this century the laws had few teeth in them, that the controls that existed were often not used, and that the courts generally interpreted laws to favor the trusts whenever possible. Average people were not apathetic toward the problem; they honestly thought that this problem was solved.[9]

Yet another reason why symbols of government are important is that they reflect people's ideas, their perceptions of the world, and sometimes their innermost thoughts. Keith Baird, for example, a Barbados-born high school teacher from Brooklyn, revealed his perception of the civil-rights struggle through his use of symbols. When Baird introduced a resolution at the national meeting of the American Federation of Teachers in 1966 urging a campaign to substitute the term "Afro-American" for "Negro," he showed clearly his perception of the civil rights movement; he argued that "it was high time that Negroes moved up to hyphenated status such as the Italian-Americans and other minority groups." "Negro" to him had historically been used "'solely to describe the enslaved and the enslavable.'"[10]

Historically there was nothing inherently distasteful about the word "Negro." It had no pejorative connotations. Neither is it generally recognized that there is a high status in being a hyphenated American. Further, if Negroes had been called Afro-Americans for two hundred years, Baird might well be arguing today that we should substitute the word "Negro." Baird's resolution, however, did reveal his attitudes toward civil rights and his profound disturbance by all aspects of racism and bigotry. And so today, because of the urgings of modern civil rights leaders, "Negro" is typically replaced by the term "black."

George Kennan, in trying to determine the perception of Asians toward the world, depended on an analysis of their political symbols. His conclusion—that Asians are less fearful of communism than we would like them to be—is founded on two arguments. First, he says, "the power of these various semantic symbols [communism, imperialism, and colonialism] is entirely different in Asia than it is in Europe." The Asians fear imperialism and colonialism, which they have fought against for two hundred years, more than they fear communism. Second, Asians are not conscious of losing "freedom" under communism. There is no freedom as we know it in many Asian and African countries today. The "Chinese language has only one word which remotely resembles our word 'freedom,' and that conveys the sense of license and rather turbulent indiscipline." [11]

It is no wonder that Lasswell wrote, "It is apparent that change in the spread and frequency of exposure to key signs is an exceedingly significant indicator of important social processes. We can follow the dissemination of secular or sacred cults by surveying trends in the geographical distribution of icons and other significant signs found in the whole complex. Similarly, we can establish the presumption of integrative or disintegrative trends within any society by observing sign frequencies." [12]

Although symbols are significant because people instinctively believe that they are important, because they can substitute for political action, and because they reflect people's innermost thoughts and ideas, symbols are also important because they determine the very way people think. Symbols not only reflect; they mold.

As trial lawyers have known for years, how a person asks a question can predetermine the answer he or she receives. [13] Appropriate words and symbols can determine not only the answer to a question, but also the way people think and the way they are able to ask their questions. For example, at the Unification Congress of July–August 1903, V. I. Lenin was able to adopt a new name for his caucus. Out of dissatisfaction with the proceedings the Bund withdrew, leaving Lenin with a small majority. The name Lenin adopted then was *Bolshinstvo* ("Majority") or *Bolsheviki* ("Majorityites").

Though but yesterday . . . he had been in a minority, and, more often than not would be in the minority in the future, he would never relinquish *the psychological advantage of that name*. A name, he knew, was a program, a distilled essence, more powerful in its impact upon the untutored mind than any propaganda slogan. What pride it could give to his caucus. No matter how it might dwindle, always to call itself "Majorityites." What conviction, what an air of legality, of democratic majority sanction, it would give in appealing to the rank and file and the non-party masses. If he had remained in a minority, he would have chosen some other banner name—like "True Iskrists" or "Orthodox Marxists" or "Revolutionary Wing of the Russian Social Democracy." But it is characteristic of the ineptness of his opponents that they permanently accepted the designation of Mensheviki (Minorityites) for their group [emphasis added].[14]

In Russia, as in the United States, it is important to join the "bandwagon" or the "wave of the future." Lenin, by preempting the label Majorityites, determined the perceptions of his audience so that they thought of Lenin's caucus as having majority sanction.

It was no accident that during the Vietnam War, the administration labeled American bombing raids into North Vietnam "protective retaliation" raids. A verb such as "to protect" has more favorable connotations than the more blunt, "to bomb." The introduction of United States troops into Laos was an "incursion," a much more limiting-sounding word than the traditional term "invasion." A retreat became a "mobile maneuver," and thus lost some of the implications of defeat. As the term "military advisors" began to acquire negative connotations, the imagemakers relabeled them "delivery team auditors."[15] To murder an enemy spy became the more antiseptic-sounding, "to terminate with extreme prejudice." And defoliation was called the more neutral "resources control program."[16] In 1968 the *Army Digest*, quoting the Judge Advocate General's Office, insisted that the fighting in Vietnam was an "international armed conflict," not a war.[17]

More recently the opponents of sex discrimination have recognized that in order to change people's attitudes toward women and their roles, it is necessary to change the words used: the head of a committee is the "chairperson"; the secretary is no longer a "girl." At first the change in words may be only symptomatic of the new attitudes toward sex discrimination. But the purpose of the verbal play is to affect future attitudes toward sexual stereotyping.

Modern linguistic research supports this theory: language in general and symbols in particular mold the manner in which people think. People think and talk by using words, and even when they think without using words but by using "ideas," language still structures their thoughts. Benjamin Whorf, after studying the language patterns of Hopi (an American Indian tongue) and some modern European languages—mainly English, French, and German—concluded that even very abstract concepts like "time" and "matter" are "not given in substantially the same form by experience to all men but depend on the nature of the language or languages through which they have been developed."[18] Another linguist, Edward Sapir, makes essentially the same observation: "Though language is not ordinarily thought of as of essential interest to the students of social science, it powerfully conditions all our thinking about social problems and processes."[19]

The Importance of the Symbol "Liberal"

Though all widespread symbols are important, certain symbols, at various times, carry particular significance. In fact, much of United States political history can be interpreted as a rivalry for the possession of certain words. In the early days of our Republic, the Hamiltonians—those in favor of a strong national government—called themselves Federalists, though at that time "federation" meant what "confederation" means today. The "true federalists" found themselves at a tactical disadvantage: they were in the position of arguing against federalism because they had accepted the label Anti-Federalist.[20]

Shortly after 1800 the value of the federal symbol declined. The decline occurred partly because the debate was over; the federal Constitution had been adopted, and few people advocated its repeal. The term also lost value because it acquired bad connotations: the rigidity of the Federalist party associated its inflexibility with the term "federalist."

"Democracy" then became a useful symbol, because the next issue on the agenda was the question of democracy. For example, in the post–Civil War Gilded Age, some argued that in a true democracy the government, not big business, should make the basic economic decisions, while the proponents of laissez faire contended that their economic doctrines represented true democracy.[21] Since virtually everyone in the United States now believes in democracy and all Republicans and Democrats are recognized to be true democrats, there is no longer any political advantage in proclaiming oneself a democrat.

While democracy is no longer the basis for rivalry in this country, in the outside world democracy is not universally a matter of faith. There, this word, together with socialism, communism, and liberalism, "are the labels which sum up the basic terms of the political contest of the nineteenth and twentieth centuries," states Giovanni Sartori.[22] In the United States, however, democracy offers its holders no great advantage, since everyone holds it. Socialism and communism are derogatory labels here, falling as they do outside the American tradition.[23] The only modern label of world importance that has also been important in this country is liberal or liberalism.

As a case study, the word "liberal" represents an important symbol to illustrate the use of political symbols and their rise and decline, because it is a peculiarly powerful word. Although liberalism has no precise meaning in this country, whenever people have tried to give it meaning they have often included themselves in the definition, or in the "true definition"[24]—at least until very recently, when "conservative" has become a much more fashionable word.[25] Whatever its meaning, no one wants to be considered illiberal in the United States. Adam Ulam claimed that everyone "in the West who is not a self-declared fascist lays claim to being a liberal of sorts and programs ranging from extreme conservatism to communism are advocated in the name of 'liberalism.'"[26] Herbert Hoover, Franklin D. Roosevelt, and Robert Taft, among many others, have all strongly claimed that they were liberals.[27] Hoover and Taft were as positive that the New Deal did not represent liberalism as Roosevelt was certain that it did. Even as the term "conservative" has become more popular, with "liberal" in the decline, the new conservatives often call themselves libertarians.

Such respect for the power of this political symbol makes itself clear "in the qualifying adjectives which those who attack 'liberals' usually take the trouble to use," says Charles Frankel.[28] Even in 1958, when President Eisenhower was campaigning for the very conservative William Knowland of California, Ike attacked the "*self-styled* liberals . . . [with] the irresistible impulse . . . to squander money—your money" (emphasis added).[29] Only the self-styled liberals are under attack; the true liberals are, by implication, fine people. One commentator has elaborated on this peculiar American habit of attacking only qualified liberals.

> Southern Senators who are proud to be known as conservatives normally train their guns not on "liberals" but on "Northern liberals." And they not infrequently add that they are themselves as liberal as the next man in matters of foreign policy or social welfare. Even the late Senator McCarthy handled the word gingerly. His memorably modulated remarks were usually studded with the phrase "phony liberals." This carried the convenient suggestion, to be sure, that all liberals were phonies. But it also left the inference open that he had nothing against genuine liberals, if he could only find any.[30]

Of course, the fact that "liberal" is a favorable political symbol in the United States does not mean that a person is at an advantage being labeled too liberal. For example, Spiro Agnew, while vice-president, attacked the "radical liberals."[31] Extremism is a vice and not a virtue for most Americans. But the unqualified symbol "liberal" is recognized by many politicians to have some political drawing power.

When we look at public opinion polls of the middle 1960s, when the liberal label was very popular, we can see that politicians were correct about the drawing power of liberalism. In one poll of the 20,546 students enrolled on the campus of Michigan State University, 42 percent declared themselves to be Democrats or leaning in that direction, and 51 percent said they were Republicans or leaning in that direction. Although this school, which is supposed to be a typical large midwestern university, was more Republican than Democratic, 53 percent of the students declared themselves to be very or moderately liberal.[32] Candidates who emphasize that they are liberal would have more drawing power than those who try to draw merely Democratic votes.

An even earlier poll also demonstrated the drawing power of the liberal symbol. After following area-sampling procedures; interviewing 3,068 respondents in California, Illinois, and New Mexico; considering only voting data for the 1944, 1946, and 1948 elections; and allowing voters to classify themselves as liberal or conservative, the pollsters concluded, "Liberalism-conservatism suggest at least a partial explanation of non-voting and of dissatisfaction of respondents from their favored party. Thus it can be inferred from our data that the liberal Republican and the conservative Democrat did not feel as much at home in their respective parties as did conservative Republicans and liberal Democrats, and they expressed their divergence by a smaller turnout at the polls and by voting less often for the candidates of their favored party."[33]

These two older polls show another important point, besides the former drawing power of the liberal symbol: in spite of the fact that many politicians of different beliefs claimed that they were liberal, the average person, at least since 1944, generally agrees as to who is liberal. When the 1962 Michigan State University Poll asked an open-ended question—who is liberal? who is conservative?—64 percent of the students picked Barry Goldwater as a known conservative and 62 percent spontaneously said that John F. Kennedy was a known liberal.[34] The second poll, based on the elections of the late 1940s, stated that in general those people who considered themselves conservative—whether they were Democrats or Republicans—thought the Republican party to be more their home than the Democratic party; those who considered themselves to be liberal felt the Democratic party to be more their home. These findings are especially important when we remember that the symbol "liberal" has to operate often as a cross-pressure against the very significant factor of party identification.

A Case Study in the Use of the Liberal Label

That most people now agree that Herbert Hoover was not a liberal does not explain why he honestly called himself a liberal until his death. And, even if we grant that Franklin D. Roosevelt was a recognized liberal of the New Deal days, what about other important figures of the New Deal? Were they liberal? Is Walter Lippmann a liberal? Is Governor LaFollette a liberal? Is Justice Black a liberal? Max Lerner says that we ask these questions with "desperate amusement" because all these men share in the liberal heritage and yet have important differences among themselves.[35] Alan P. Grimes, after considering the very different men who have called themselves liberal, asks, "Must we then despair of definition? Is a liberal nothing more than any man who calls himself one? Or is called one?"[36] Grimes answers "no" to this question and then tries to classify the concepts that form his definition of liberalism. Any such definition, however, is by its nature normative and not descriptive; such a definition excludes many people who claim to be liberal and have convinced others that they are liberal.

For the purpose of this case study, I will use a very descriptive, functional, and operational definition: a person is a liberal who can convince other people that he or she is a liberal. Given this definition, which does not arbitrarily exclude anyone from being labeled liberal, the immediate question one should ask is why Roosevelt came to be identified as a liberal and Hoover did not. Both were self-declared liberals. Given that both Hoover and Roosevelt honestly considered themselves to be liberal, and that "liberal" is a potent political symbol with which many politicians have wanted to identify, why is there now a general consensus that Hoover was no liberal? Why was it that Hoover was so unsuccessful in capturing this word?

An immediate answer to such questions would probably

assume that usage in the United States of the political symbol "liberal" has generally followed British usage. Given this assumption, one could explain that British liberalism has, over the years, changed its meaning, especially with L. T. Hobhouse's formulation of a new liberalism in 1911.[37] This new British liberalism tried to establish a middle course between socialism and classical liberalism. The new British welfare liberals, says Thomas P. Neill, "insisted against the socialists that wealth was produced by individual initiative, and they insisted against the individualists that the site value of real property depended almost entirely on the community, that the right of ownership to even personal property was meaningless without social approval and maintenance."[38] In line with this new liberalism, Winston Churchill, while a member of the Liberal party, argued in 1908 that he "should like to see the state undertaking new functions, stepping forward into new spheres of activity, particularly in services which are in the nature of monopolies."[39] These new English liberals still believed in liberty, but they also believed that the right to a living wage was as important a liberty as the right to property and personal liberty.[40] Further, they believed that the state could pass laws to ensure the former without denying the latter liberty.[41]

Given this background, Herbert Hoover would have had to overthrow a generation of opinion to persuade people to accept his nineteenth-century laissez-faire definition of liberalism. Hence, it was to be expected that he would fail to capture this favorable political label.

However, this immediate answer makes a very important but incorrect assumption: that the United States had followed English use of the political symbol "liberal"; that for thirty years the great majority of Americans knew what "liberal" meant; and that therefore Hoover and his conservative contemporaries tried to steal this important symbol of the New Deal. Yet all available evidence suggests that "liberal" was not an important political symbol in the United States until the 1930s. This is not to say that "liberal" was never used before the New Deal; rather, it was not an important *symbol* before the New Deal. For the great majority of Americans, the word "liberal" was literally born in the early New Deal.

The term "liberal" was not a favorite American political label of earlier eras. An examination of the political symbols used in some early political literature demonstrates this fact. Herbert Croly's book, *The Promise of American Life*, is certainly one of these books. It was first published in November 1909 and was reprinted in June 1910 and April 1911. Although at that time it did not sell more than 7,500 copies, Arthur Schlesinger, Jr., states that "it had immediate and extensive influence on what historians have come to call the Progressive era."[42] To add to Croly's liberal credentials, I should also point out that he founded the *New Republic*. Yet, after analyzing the symbols used in *The Promise*, Samuel H. Beer concluded: "Only occasionally in this book . . . he uses the term liberal or liberalism. No more frequently he used conservatism—but in a formula that opposed it to radicalism. The term with which he, like his hero Theodore Roosevelt, identified himself and his views, was, of course, 'progressivism.'"[43]

Croly's infrequent use of the term "liberal" is made even more dramatic if we briefly compare the Democratic Roosevelt's use of the term. In the first volume of Roosevelt's public papers, representing the years 1928 to 1932, there are no references to "liberalism" in the index. Yet a few years later we find that FDR titles Volume 7, representing the year 1938, *The Continuing Struggle for Liberalism*.[44] A dramatic shift had taken place in FDR's vocabulary—a shift that was not foreseen in the political terminology of Croly's *The Promise*.

In the pre-Croly era, in the eighteenth century, Beer observes that "generic terms—such as 'democratic'—are used in addition to party labels to designate important viewpoints. But 'liberal' is not among them."[45] One cannot argue that "liberal" was never used but rather that in quantitative terms this symbol was insignificant. A review of political symbols in popular magazines[46] and newspapers[47] also demonstrates that the increased use of the liberal label coincided with the New Deal.

Some of the more important figures of the early New Deal also recall that it was during this period that the word "liberal" became an important political symbol. Raymond Moley writes that on March 8, 1933, he prepared Roosevelt's message that went to Congress on March 10. In this speech Moley remembers using the expression "liberal."[48] "The word 'liberal' in its present meaning was then only beginning to supplant the old word 'progressive.'"[49] Arthur Krock of the *New York Times*, also a very politically aware actor of the New Deal era, says that he agrees with Moley that around 1933 "liberalism" started to replace "progressivism."[50] A very influential brain-truster, Rexford G. Tugwell, also remembers that "liberalism" emerged as an important political symbol in the time of Franklin Delano Roosevelt.[51] Tugwell, in fact, describes the New Deal as "a time of confusion, of trying to attain collectivistic organization under individualistic labels."[52]

Not until the early 1930s did "liberal" become a very important political symbol. This symbol had been used before in American history, but never in any significant way. Then suddenly politicians, publicists, and articulate people in general began expressing themselves and thinking in terms of this new label. In the 1930s there was a great debate in America over whether Hoover or FDR properly owned the symbol. Even long after the New Deal, the very conservative John T. Flynn, refusing to admit defeat, pleaded in Hoover-like language for the Hoover-like argument that "the Communist, the fascist and the planner, who is really a fascist, have reversed all this. [Previously, the central state was the enemy of liberalism.] They propose to make the State more powerful than ever with its arsenal of economic weapons. They call this the dream of liberalism. *I say they have stolen a grand old word and are running amuck with their plundered property*" (emphasis added).[53]

The symbol "liberal" is especially important for the New Deal period because, as it emerged, it seemed to represent something new. The new symbol implied new action. Second, the new symbol and the debate it caused reflected the intellectual turmoil of a nation trying to decide whether to accept or reject a new deal in politics. Third, this new symbol, unlike a geographical term, allowed people to think in terms of classes, not sections of the country —that is, to think in liberal-conservative terms and not in northern-southern terms. Finally, this symbol was especially important for people who lived at the time of the New Deal because they thought that the debate over who owned the new liberal label was an important debate. In fact, by 1936 the editors of the *New York Times*, reflecting public concern, could write that the fight for the liberal label "is coming forward as an issue in the national campaign. Both New Deal and anti-administration spokesmen declare their devotion to the liberal ideal of freedom and democracy; both assail each other as opponents of true liberalism." [54]

We may grant that symbols are important; that the symbol "liberal" is especially important in the United States; and that by the end of the 1930s "liberal" had become a viable symbol used to identify New Deal programs. Yet the birth and maturation of the liberal label raises more difficult questions. How and why did this political symbol gain such wide usage in the United States in such a short period of time? Why did this symbol remain viable when others such as New Freedom, New Deal, Normalcy, and more recent ones such as Fair Deal and New Frontier are now anachronistic? Did FDR choose the symbol "liberal" to designate his programs? How consciously did he make this choice? If FDR did choose the symbol, why did he choose *it* and not some other symbol such as "progressive"? How was Roosevelt able to convince the public that he, and not Hoover, was the "true liberal"? In the period during which both Hoover and Roosevelt claimed that they were each liberal, how confused was the public? And why, in more recent times, did the liberal label decline in importance, as more politicians unabashedly began to call themselves conservative?

This study seeks to determine how and why this viable political symbol emerged, what the public's attitude was toward it, and how powerful this symbol was at the time of the New Deal. Why did this symbol rise in importance, and why did it decline? After studying the British analogy, the American background until the debate of the 1930s, the great debate itself, and post-1940 attitudes toward liberalism, we should be in a much better position to determine the answers to these questions. These conclusions should then enable us to understand the importance and usefulness, in the legal and political arenas, of symbols generally.

2

The British Analogy

The Emergence of Liberalism in England

Giovanni Sartori correctly observes that "while the *thing* liberalism has been—according to Harold Laski, an unimpeachable witness—the outstanding doctrine of the West for four centuries, the *word* is much more recent."[1] Liberalism was conceived in 1811 when a group of Spaniards proposed the adoption of a new constitution based on the French constitution of 1781, which in turn was based on the radical thought of *les philosophes*. The proponents of this radical constitution called themselves Liberales, and because the origins of the Liberales were in the Enlightenment, their thought included anticlericalism as an essential ingredient from the very beginning.[2]

The Liberales became even more anticlerical in their debate over the new constitution with the monarchists and the clerical and lay supporters of the Catholic church; these opponents of the Liberales condemned the constitution as an unworkable document based on false theological and philosophical assumptions.[3] While the Spanish right wing was certainly not admirable, one could hardly consider these new Spanish Liberales paragons of virtue, either. Thomas P. Neill has called their philosophy "doctrinaire, as only the Spanish can be doctrinaire; arbitrary, and, paradoxically, quite illiberal."[4]

From Spain the term "liberal" traveled to Italy, appearing as *liberalismo*, and to France, as *liberalisme*, where it was used to describe certain local political beliefs.[5] It is important to realize that in each case the new label was being applied to beliefs that already existed. The term "liberalism" came after the thing liberalism had been born and—since the word followed the fact—

there was no necessity for any ideological similarities in the different countries' use of the term. In some countries—for example, Germany—"people began to speak of 'liberalism' when they had ceased, or were ceasing, to be liberal."⁶ Although it turned out that liberalism in the Latin countries generally implied anticlericalism, there was nothing in the label "liberal" that required this relationship to exist. In fact, although English liberalism had some theological implications, it was not really anticlerical; its concerns were primarily economic and secondarily political.⁷

The manner in which the term "liberalism" took root in England from the Continent is especially instructive. From 1811 to 1830 the term "liberalism" had been traveling around the Continent acquiring connotations of revolution, anticlericalism, arbitrariness—in short, what Americans today would generally call extremism. Then, around 1830, the left wing of the Whig party combined with Radicals and businessmen to campaign for what was to become the Reform Bill of 1832, a proposal to extend the franchise to include the business class and to redistrict the country in order to give the growing industrial centers a fairer representation.⁸ Macaulay called it "this second Bill of Rights, this Greatest Charter of the Liberties of England," but the landowners did not favor a second Magna Carta that would reduce the powers that they had obtained from the first one.

It is difficult for us now—in an age where even the most totalitarian regimes pay lip service to democracy—to appreciate exactly how worried the landed gentry really was. Their worry turned to outright fear when Daniel O'Connell suggested carrying the proposed reform even further, to include a secret ballot and universal male suffrage. The *Annual Register* attacked his idea as being based on the "simple, but mad proposition, that every man who pays a tax, or is liable to serve in the militia, is entitled to have a voice in the representation."⁹ The *Annual Register* should not have been so frightened, because the left-wing Whigs and the businessmen believed that only the middle class with sufficient property should have the vote. However, under either the Reform Bill of 1832 or O'Connell's proposed amendment to that reform, the landowners would lose considerable power, and they opposed the reform vehemently.¹⁰

As one method of opposing the reform, the landed gentry and their representatives in Parliament, the Tories, decided to achieve what they thought would be the strategic advantage of calling their opponents "liberals," thereby (the Tories hoped) identifying them with the "un-English" revolutionaries of the Continent.[11] "Liberal" in England, then, was first applied with the intention of being a derogatory term.

But "liberal" seemed to be a word with inherently good implications. In England, since before 1600, the adjective "liberal" has meant "free from prejudice or orthodox zeal."[12] "Liberal" implies "liberality" and "liberty"; all these words are derived from the same Latin word: *liber*, meaning "free."

In another era, the Roman government had found *liberalitas*—meaning "liberality"—a very good symbol to place on their coins as a method of winning and retaining political support from the people.[13] As Thomas P. Neill correctly observes, "'Liberty' is a beautiful word in any language. Its connotations have always been appealing, noble, high-minded. . . . The adjective 'liberal' imputes loftiness of view, concern with the things of the spirit, a respect for human decency. 'Illiberal,' on the other hand, is a word of ugly connotations. It implies smallness of soul, pettiness of outlook, selfishness of nature. Everyone, then, wants to be considered liberal in this sense."[14]

"Liberal" was a particularly favorable symbol for the advanced Whigs because of the moment at which it was introduced. Over the entire Continent there was agitation for reform. The word captured this drift of modern history, for it implied liberty, removal of restraint, and progress.[15] In nineteenth-century England, "liberal" was an advantageous word to use for political purposes. The advanced Whigs did exactly that; because the adjective "liberal" had such laudatory implications in England—regardless of Continental ferment—they readily accepted the so-called un-English, foreign label "liberal."[16]

The opponents of the new liberal wing of the Whig party were at an obvious disadvantage. Not only did their plan to attach the term "liberal" to the advanced Whigs as a derogatory label backfire, but their own appellation, "Tory," was considered a reproachful designation at that time. Then J. W. Croker, in an article dated January 1, 1830, used a new label: "conservative." He used this term in a political sense, meaning the maintenance of existing political and ecclesiastical institutions. Many Tories who had disapproved of old Tory reaction immediately began showing preference for the new term, "conservative."[17]

The new liberals thought that "conservative" was not as proper a word for their opponents as the pejorative "Tory," so at first the liberals ridiculed this new label.[18] However, at that time there was a shift not only in party names but also in party principles. The liberal Whigs, fighting for the middle class rather than the farmers or laborers, began to draw support from many Tories who were manufacturers or members of the educated middle class. For a while there were three major groups in Parliament: the Tories, the Whigs, and the Liberals. "The traditional parliamentary system seemed unable to admit by the side of the Whig and Tory parties a third not reducible to either," says Guido De Ruggiero. "But in time the more active and vital mentality of the free trade party drew the antiquated Liberalism of the Whigs into its own orbit and so restored the old two-party system, though giving its form a new content."[19] The old content was a contest between two parties, both of which were based on a single aristocratic tradition, and both of which were grounded in the same privileges of birth. The new content was politics based on class interest.[20] And so the new division in Parliament was no longer Whig/Tory but instead Liberal/Conservative.[21]

Because the new party names reflected a fundamental change in political substance, they proved durable. Since the new Liberals represented different policies and drew their support from the middle class—because, in short, they were not really Whigs—it made sense for people to call them liberal. And since the new Conservatives were more than just Tories, this label also proved lasting, even though the Liberals argued that the new Conservatives should continue to be called Tories.

The Conservatives in England had lost the chance to be called liberal. Though they tried often to become associated with the word,[22] it became the name of a politically distinct party, the Liberal party. Hence, in England the political label could have a fairly precise meaning; "liberal" was not so vague an appellation that many different people of different parties could attach themselves to it.

The Elements of English Liberalism
and the Seeds of Change

That "liberalism" was attached to one of England's two major parties and thus had a fairly specific political meaning did not imply that the definition of liberalism could not change. There were three basic elements of classical liberalism that contained within themselves the seeds of welfare liberalism: the Radical element, the economic element, and the religious element.[23]

The primary representative of Radical thought was Jeremy Bentham. Bentham was extremely efficient, extremely individualistic, extremely rationalistic, and extremely cold. It was said of him that he "sinned against the imagination." Ruggiero states, "All law is to him an evil, because an infraction of the liberty of the individual; and, in general, every function of government is an evil."[24]

Bentham believed that society is in harmony when people act according to their self-interest. However, sometimes individuals do not follow their self-interest. Hence, government is justified in passing laws to prevent them from following a false self-interest and thus infringing on another's liberty. But there is no such thing as natural law; rather, all law is made by government and all law properly "draws its inspiration from the interest of the greatest number, as against a narrowly selfish interest falsely so called."[25]

Bentham's principle was readily adopted by the bourgeoisie, who used it against the selfishness of the landowning class. The manufacturers were not the only ones, however, who could use Bentham's principles. Although radicalism was in part a liberal, middle-class philosophy, in the sense that the self-interest principle meant individualism and protection of individual liberties, radicalism could also be democratic, since the happiness of the greatest number was the justification of laws. Also within Bentham's philosophy was the seed of welfare and socialism: if the workers received the franchise, the state —in the name of the greatest-happiness principle and uninhibited by thoughts of natural property rights—could be very socialistic.[26]

We can more easily see the capacity for welfare liberalism and even socialism in Bentham's principles if we quickly turn to John Ruskin's *Unto This Last*, one of the most influential books for British politics at the turn of the century. According to John D. Rosenburg, "Clement Attlee, who became a socialist after reading the works of Ruskin and William Morris, wrote that the modern Labour Party was born in 1906, when twenty-nine independent Labourites were returned to the House of Commons; according to a questionnaire circulated among them, the book which most profoundly influenced their thoughts was *Unto This Last*."[27] Yet the same author who was so influential with the first members of England's great socialist party was able to argue consistently that the political economy should strive for "the greatest number of human beings noble and happy."[28]

The second major element of classical liberalism that had within it this germ of welfare liberalism was the philosophy of the Economists. The Economists were related to the Benthamite Radicals, but they were also descendants of Adam Smith. Smith's followers believed in *homo oeconomicus* but then kept him in a laboratory. Economic Man was not sent "into the streets like a man of flesh and blood to make laws for his fellow men."[29] The second important distinction between the Radicals and the Economists was that these descendants of Adam Smith did not believe in natural harmony if all people would follow their self-interest. Instead they believed in inevitable conflict in society.

Malthus voiced one aspect of this conflict in his *Essay on Population*. A large population, he declared, is not always good. He thought that the increase in population was much faster than the proportional increase in production of food from land. The group responsible for the misery caused by the overproduction of people was the laboring class. He seemed to be saying to the workers, "Your . . . lack of self-control has led you to multiply to the point of murderous mutual competition."[30] Ricardo took Malthus's argument one step further. His villain was not the proletariat but the landowner. More land would have to be farmed as the population increased. Also, since some lands were more fertile than others, the more fertile lands would increase in value as the population grew. The few landowners who had the good fortune to own these more fertile lands would become wealthy merely by waiting; such landowners would grow richer without working any harder.

The industrial bourgeoisie used Ricardo's theory to show that not they but the landowners were the selfish members of society responsible for the workers' misery. Yet this argument of the business interests still had within it the seeds of welfare: if the land's value is created by society, then society should obviously own the land. Expropriate the villains! Says De Ruggiero, "The working man soon . . . quoted Ricardo against Ricardo." [31]

The American Henry George was one major figure who used Ricardo's argument to justify exclusive state possession of rent. George believed that Ricardo's law of rent was a "geometric axiom." He argued that rent, because it increases faster than the productive power of labor and capital, forces down wages and interest, thereby causing depressions and more poverty. George's simple solution to the problem was to have the state appropriate rent. With the continually increasing revenues from the single tax on land, the state could operate a whole new set of programs. He predicted, "We would reach the ideal of the socialist but not through government repression. Government would become the administration of a great co-operative society." [32]

The third major element of classical liberalism that had within it the seeds of change was the religious one. Religious Nonconformity, Gladstone had said, was "the backbone of British Liberalism." Individual initiative, competition, and the spirit of Calvinism were in each of the Nonconformist sects. Their organization was congregational and their members were, in the main, drawn from the middle class and the elite of the working class. [33] These revived Nonconformist sects served to make radicalism more humane. The *homo oeconomicus* and the Good Samaritan became bedfellows. Parallel to Nonconformity, which was inspired by Methodism, was the Evangelical movement, which worked within the Church of England and produced many of the same moral and social results of Methodism.

The result of these religious developments, said John Dewey, was that there was a general humanitarian movement "instigated by religion [that] was active in attack upon slavery, upon the abuses of prison life, upon brutal and mechanical methods of administering charity, and through the factory laws, upon the inhuman conditions of labor of women and children in mines and factories. In every one of these movements evangelical zeal was the motive force."[34] This humanitarian zeal was, of course, the seed of a new liberalism.

By the end of the 1860s, the Classical Liberal party had opposed the Crimean War, eventually favored the North in the American Civil War (because the liberals saw the North fighting against slavery), cut government budgets, instituted direct taxes, encouraged more independence of the colonies—which in turn paved the way for a Commonwealth—and encouraged religious freedom. But the Liberal party as yet had no education policy; they opposed the Factory Acts and state protection for workers; and they had a pedantic reverence for freedom of contract which operated greatly to the advantage of the owners of the means of production.[35]

The Seeds of the New Liberalism Grow, Mature, and Wither

As we have seen, the liberal label had a fairly precise meaning in England because it was associated with a definite political party. Yet this fairly precise meaning was able to develop because the doctrine of liberalism had within it the seeds of change. Simply because seeds are planted, however, does not assure that they will grow; there must be an appropriate climate. England after around 1870 supplied that climate.

One of the most important climatic changes was the different attitude of the workers. Many liberals had argued that poverty is incurable. However, since industrialized England was quite prosperous, it became increasingly difficult to convince the poor that their poverty was natural. Many argued that "if 'natural laws' of economics condemned them to poverty in a prosperous milieu, then it was time to adopt a system with different laws of operation."[36] The workers took the three major elements of classical liberalism outlined in the previous section and carried the arguments within them to their logical conclusion.

The workers also adopted and developed the other arguments

of classical liberalism: the majority rule and universal suffrage implicit in extending the franchise; emphasizing the freedom of their jobs more than the freedom of trade; the individual liberty to organize politically and economically as workers. They wanted economic progress, but by progress they meant humankind's collective control over economic life.[37]

What the workers thought was now more important because they had the vote. The Conservatives had advocated labor legislation and a widened franchise in order to capture the labor vote, which they proceeded to do for a time. Hence, after the second electoral reform of 1867, the Conservatives were able to defeat Gladstone's cabinet in 1874.[38] The Conservatives' more benevolent attitude pressured the Liberals to change, in order to be able to recapture power. In 1884 it was the Liberal government that tried to win labor's votes by extending the suffrage to rural workers, thus making adult male suffrage almost universal.[39]

Not only were the workers' attitudes changing, but the liberals' attitudes were also changing, a shift prompted in part by the need to win workers' votes. Another reason for the change was simply that the society of small capitalists that the liberal philosophy postulated no longer existed. In response to the new large corporations, unions grew up.[40] Eventually liberals began to realize that unions were an appropriate form of organization because they were spontaneous bodies of free workers and because they enabled workers to compete on equal terms.[41] Many liberals also began to realize that because of the growing complexities of society—education, public works, banking activities, railways, and shipping companies—all these activities were taking on the functions of public services and therefore should be regulated, controlled, or owned by the state.[42] Since the time of Bentham, liberals had used the legislature to enact reform; thus many liberals were not shocked when they found themselves using the legislature in a positive manner.[43]

We can most easily see this dramatic shift in the meaning of "liberal" if we look briefly at the effects of that shift in John Stuart Mill. Mill was at first the loyal follower of Bentham. He wrote *Utilitarianism* primarily to defend Bentham's "greatest happiness principle," and in the course of that defense he modified that doctrine in order to make it more powerful. Yet this same Mill could write, by the end of his life, that even if he would suddenly achieve all the changes in institutions and opinions that his utilitarian philosophy desired, he would still not be happy.

After utilitarianism gave him a mental crisis, Mill decided to abandon that cold philosophy of the radicals: "If I am asked, what system of political philosophy I substituted for that which, as a philosophy, I had abandoned, I answer, No system: only a conviction that the true system was something much more complex and many-sided than I had previously had any idea of."[44] This same Mill also surprisingly concluded, "If the choice were to be made between communism with all its chances, and the present state of society with all its sufferings and injustices, if this, or communism, were the alternative, all the difficulties great or small of communism would be as dust in the balance."[45]

In short, liberalism was changing. The philosophy that was adequate in the first half of the nineteenth century in England was no longer tolerable in the second half. The major philosophers of liberalism, exemplified by J. S. Mill, changed their beliefs in response to the new situation, and the seeds of change thrived in the new climate.

Old classical liberalism was poured out of the bottle and welfare liberalism was poured in; but although the contents were new, the label "liberalism" was not changed. Since welfare liberalism grew out of basic elements of classical liberalism, it seemed reasonable to many that the same label would be used to describe both philosophies.

However reasonable the retention of the old label was, we must remember that liberalism had already shown itself to be a very important symbol for members of a political party to use. Therefore we would expect that those proponents of classical liberalism would object to the capture of this symbol by the advocates of a welfare state. They did indeed object.

The major representative of the Manchester liberals, who did not want to lose their liberal label, was Herbert Spencer. Spencer was such a great believer in laissez faire that he even wanted private enterprise to run the highway and sewer systems. Spencer agreed that quack doctors could cause the loss of life, but to use the state to forbid them to practice "is directly to violate the moral law."[46] This very inflexible classical liberal strongly objected in 1884 that the new so-called liberalism was in reality a kind of Toryism, since it had given up the idea of the freedom of contract and voluntary cooperation that distinguished it from a "coercive military organization."[47] To protect their label from misuse, says Thomas P. Neill, Spencer and the other Manchester liberals formed "the Liberty and Property Defense League, much like the American Liberty League of 1934, that set forth on a crusade to defend liberty and property from the attacks of the new 'welfare' liberalism. . . . Each group laid claim to the title liberalism and accused the other of 'spurious liberalism' or 'blind conservatism.'"[48]

There were two major reasons why Spencer failed to recapture the liberal label. First, it was quite logical for the welfare liberals to be called liberal, since their beliefs about welfare grew out of the elements of classical liberalism. Second, "liberal" had been historically associated in England with the name of a political party. When the new liberals won control of the party, they won control of the label. Those who clung to the tenets of laissez faire were simply read out of the party. The protesters were called "conservative."[49]

The new welfare liberalism developed and eventually stood for a whole period of social progress. For example, before World War I there was a burst of social reform under the Campbell-Bannerman and Asquith governments that was "in many ways like the New Deal and in fact providing specific models for some of its legislation."[50] By the second decade of this century, the transition to this new liberalism was complete. It was now a fairly mature doctrine. The welfare liberals in general saw themselves as beyond the era of the Manchester school. In political beliefs they saw themselves as between the Tories and the Socialists. They were the middle road.

Hobhouse explained how the new liberalism went beyond the beliefs of laissez faire: "If we grant . . . that it is demanded of all sane adult men and women that they should live as civilized beings, as industrious workers, as good parents, as orderly and efficient citizens, it is, on the other side, the function of the economic organization of society to secure them the material means of living such a life . . . and if they are not secure without the deliberate action of the state, they must be secured by the deliberate action of the state."[51] Liberalism also distinguished itself from Toryism; as Chamberlain explained, the Tories allowed intervention because of "patronage" while the Liberals intervened because they believed "all people shall be assisted to govern themselves."[52]

The new liberalism was also distinct from socialism because, as Churchill explained in 1908, "Socialism seeks to put down wealth; Liberalism would preserve private interests in the only way in which they can be safely and justly preserved, namely, by reconciling them with public right. Socialism would kill enterprise; Liberalism would rescue enterprise from the trammels of privilege and preference. Socialism assails the pre-eminence of the individual; Liberalism seeks, and shall seek more in the future, to build up a minimum standard for the mass. Socialism exalts the rule; Liberalism exalts the man. Socialism attacks capital; Liberalism attacks monopoly."[53]

Meanwhile the Labour party had been formed in 1891 and rapidly made progress.[54] The workers understood Churchill's distinction between socialism and liberalism, and they chose socialism. Although when "liberal" was first introduced into England it proved itself to be an advantageous political symbol, by the 1920s the word had lost some of its natural power because it was so connected with the Liberal party. The word had come to be the party platform. When the voters rejected the platform, they rejected the symbol that stood for the platform. By the time the New Deal was appearing in America, the electoral support of the Liberal party in England was withering.

John Maynard Keynes tried to bring new life into the Liberal party. In the late 1920s and in the early 1930s he was proposing new policies that the Liberal party should adopt. Though these policies failed to resurrect the Liberal party in Britain, it is of interest to consider Keynes's pleas. He argued that he could never bring himself to be a Conservative because "they offer me . . . neither intellectual nor spiritual consolation." What some Conservatives stood for "promotes neither my self-interest or the public good." Neither could he become a member of the Labour party because it was a class party, "and the class is not my class. . . . The *Class* war will find me on the side of the educated *bour-*

geoisie." [55] By the process of elimination, "the Liberal Party is still the best instrument of future progress—if only it had strong leadership and the right programme." [56]

An important part of this right program was of course the economic program. Keynes warned his contemporaries: "The transition from economic anarchy to a regime which deliberately aims at controlling and directing economic forces in the interests of social justice and social stability, will present enormous difficulties both technical and political. I suggest, nevertheless, that the true destiny of New Liberalism is to seek their solution." [57]

Keynes saw the Liberal party as the true middle ground for controlling economic forces. On the one side of it was fascism and on the other bolshevism. Socialism and conservatism offered no middle course: "Just as the Conservative Party will always have its Die-Hard wing, so the Labour Party will be always flanked by the Party of Catastrophe—Jacobins, Communists, Bolshevists, whatever you choose to call them." Keynes placed his hopes with the Liberal party, "the home of Economic Individualism and Social Liberty." [58]

Lessons from English History

This brief analysis of the history of the political term "liberal" in England enables us to draw some important conclusions for the study of the American symbol "liberal." In the first place, "liberal"—even before it had a chance to acquire a political meaning—had shown itself to have inherently good connotations in the English language. Even when, in 1830, the symbol was used in a derogatory sense, the naturally favorable connotations of the word easily triumphed over the pejorative foreign implications. Since both the British and Americans speak the same language, we can assume that "liberal" by itself—that is, at the introduction of the political symbol, before it has had a chance to acquire historical connotations through years of use—is also a very favorable word for a politician to capture.

The word in England also showed itself to be a fairly durable political symbol. Its permanence can be attributed to the fact that the introduction of "liberal" and "conservative" were accompanied by policy changes and the introduction of class politics. Because the new labels stood for something new, they became fairly permanent and would not easily become anachronistic.

In addition, the label "liberal" in England had had a fairly precise political meaning, because it was the actual name of a party. When the party carried the liberal doctrine to its logical conclusion and adopted a welfare program, the party also carried with it the label "liberal." Spencer's objections proved futile partly because the new liberalism grew out of the old; to apply the same name to both philosophies was logical. Spencer also failed to prevent the shift in the meaning of "liberal" because the New Liberals won control of the party, legitimating the capture of the symbol. In the United States, because no major party is called the Liberal party, we would expect the label "liberal" to be much more vague. Since there is no party platform to pour meaning into the liberal label, we would also expect that controversies surrounding its proper use would not be settled easily.

Keeping in mind the conclusions drawn from this background study of the liberal symbol in England, we can now turn to the study of the symbol in the United States.

3

The United States Background until 1932

Liberalism in the United States, 1776–1870

As explained in Chapter 1, "liberal" did not become a viable or important political symbol in America until the introduction of the New Deal. However, while the liberal label was imported here without any historical connotations,[1] like a courier without luggage, the term had still been used sporadically in the United States before 1932. This chapter analyzes these scattered uses of the term in order to determine why this particular symbol was chosen at particular times in the past; why the label did not become important in any of these past instances; and what—if any—general meaning was given to "liberal" in these past cases.

As noted in the previous chapter, "liberal" in a political sense did not even appear in the English language until 1830. When, around 1800, Hamilton advocated "a liberal construction of the Constitution,"[2] he was arguing for a loose or free construction; that is, he used "liberal" in the grammatical sense, as an adjective, and did not imply that it represented a clear, or even a vague, collection of political beliefs.

After 1830, in spite of the fact the British Tories had introduced "liberal" into the English language as a political symbol, Americans still used the term sparingly and without any real meaning. Some educated Americans, aware of politics abroad, borrowed the term; but they used it not as an American political label, but to identify their beliefs with those of Continental or British liberals. This was why Orestes Brownson called himself a liberal for a few years,[3] for at this time period the term "liberal" was insignificant as an American political symbol.

The Liberal Republicans, 1870–1872

The first and the only important national political movement before the New Deal that made definite and continued use of the symbol "liberal" was the Liberal Republican party.

History does not remember Ulysses S. Grant as one of our more adept presidents, for as his administration dragged on he made more and more enemies among independents and within the Republican ranks. In 1870 the disaffection with Grant and his policies became so serious that a new party, the Liberal Republican party, was formed. There are two questions about the Liberal Republican party that concern us: Why did it call itself Liberal Republican? And why did the symbol and the movement quickly pass into history? If we can understand what conditions cause the symbol "liberal" to be quickly forgotten, then we will have a better idea of what conditions must exist in order for the label to become viable, lasting, and significant.

The Republicans who bolted their party adopted the label "liberal" largely, I believe, because of the influence of Carl Schurz. By the middle of Grant's first term in office, there were pockets of Republican unrest all over the country, but it was Schurz's Missouri that gave birth to the actual split in the party. It was in Missouri, argues one student of the period, "that factional strife led most directly to a national Liberal movement."[4] The two leaders of Liberal Republicanism in Missouri were B. Gratz Brown[5] and Carl Schurz, an "efficient champion of the cause."[6]

It is easy enough to understand why Schurz and his followers called themselves Liberal *Republicans*. Although Schurz disagreed with many Republican policies, he had hoped to prevent a break with the administration.[7] For example, in the Missouri political campaign of 1870, an address written by Schurz characterized his faction as the "true Republican party" of Missouri. Schurz apparently considered himself a Republican, but President Grant "could see nothing but party treason in the actions of the Liberals."[8]

Why the Schurz faction called itself *Liberal* Republican is a more difficult question. The group could have continued to call themselves "true Republicans"; in fact, a minor revolt of dissatisfied Republicans in Virginia in 1869 had called themselves the "True Republicans" as the only party label.[9] Perhaps Schurz realized that it would have been a tactical error to adopt "True Republican" as the only party label. "True Republican" is not that easily distinguished from "Republican": "true" is not really descriptive, and it does not sound like a party name. Such a name would also have prompted much useless debate over who the true Republicans were. The discussion of real issues would then have been ignored.

The other label that presented itself to Schurz was "Liberal Republican." In Arkansas, also in 1869, a faction of the Republican party that was later to become the basis of support for the national Liberal Republican party had taken the name Liberal Republican party. This Arkansas faction was composed of members of the legislature who were "'old Whigs and disaffected Republicans.'"[10] Since the old American Whigs had borrowed their label from Britain, it is not surprising that in later years these Whigs would once again turn to Britain and borrow the new label that many former British Whigs owned.

The "liberal" tag of the Arkansas faction must have immediately appealed to Schurz, a liberal German who was an active participant in the revolution of 1848/49. This appeal was probably reinforced because Schurz identified his free trade position with British Liberal party policy. Schurz was one of the leading members of the American Free Trade League, formed in 1869 to encourage tariff reduction.[11] Not only Schurz but also Missouri Liberal Republicans in general favored free trade:

> The action of the tariff seemed an especial challenge to the reformers. The forcing out of David A. Wells, a conspicuous figure in the reform group, from the position of special revenue agent was resented as a victory for the protected interests in Congress. As a result the attacks on the citadel of protection became more persistent than ever. In

1870 the Free Trade League waged a most aggressive campaign. . . . The Liberal Republican campaign in Missouri that fall was in part a free-trade demonstration. Governor McClurg, the regular Republican candidate, was said to have been one of the objectionable high tariff men marked for defeat. Grosvenor, of the *Missouri Democrat*, was an ardent free-trader (the author of the League's publication, "Does Protection Protect?"), and he put forward this issue so prominently in the Liberal program that the *New York Tribune* characterized the whole Missouri movement as a free-trade conspiracy.[12]

Schurz also may have taken on this label because he understood the favorable connotations of the word. Schurz certainly used the symbol "liberal" as if he understood its power, for in the election of 1870, the Missouri Liberal Republicans "issued an address, written by Schurz, in which they unsparingly arraigned the Radicals [the Republican faction opposing the Liberals] for their *illiberality*, party trickery, and corruption in office; and they claimed themselves to represent the true Republican party of Missouri" (emphasis added).[13]

Certainly no one likes to be attacked as illiberal, but those who opposed the Liberal Republicans were, by implication and direct charge, exactly that. We would expect that the Radical Republicans would object to being labeled illiberal; in fact, when we examine the editorial pages of the *New York Times* in the days immediately preceding the election of 1872—the year of the first and last Liberal Republican presidential campaign—we quickly justify the reasonableness of our expectation.

In 1872 the *Times* was Republican and strongly supported Grant for president. In accordance with this support, they conducted an unrestrained, vituperative attack against the Liberal nominee, Horace Greeley. In the five-day period under study, whenever the *Times* called the Greeley supporters "liberal," they would very often place the word within quotation marks, implying that these "liberals" were not really liberal, that their label was an improper designation.[14]

The *Times* also tried to counteract the implication that the Liberal Republicans were a better type of Republicans: while the paper referred to the Greeley supporters as liberals eleven times in this five-day period, they called them Liberal Republicans only twice. Once they even called them Liberal Democrats! All in all, the favorite method the Radical Republicans, whom the paper favored, used to meet the challenge of their opponents' adoption of a favorable symbol was to try to avoid using it and to find another label. In the period under study, the *Times* called their opponents liberal eleven times, while they associated them in some way with Greeley (Greeleyites, Greeleyism, or Greelevites) twenty-six times. Since—as we shall soon see—the name Greeley had some very unfavorable connotations, the *Times* battled symbols with symbols.

We now come to the second question. Why did the Liberal Republican movement and the liberal symbol very quickly and unceremoniously fade into history? The first reason was that the only common factor uniting all Liberal Republicans was their universal hatred of Grant.[15] Although Schurz's belief in a free trade policy, shared with the Missouri faction, was an important factor in naming the movement, it was not an important factor in determining who would compose the national party bolt. In fact, Horace Greeley himself was a protectionist,[16] and his nomination served to alienate many of the more ardent free-traders. A great weakness of the Liberal Republicans was that their different motives for bolting produced constant disagreements. The former secretary of the Liberal Republican National Committee complained a few days before the election of 1872:

> Our party was made up of a "shake hands across the chasm" of all the soreheads and disaffected elements of the United States. It may be it would have taken superior generalship to have half the Secessionists, and Union Leaguers, and Pro-slavery men, and Abolitionists, and new Nationalists and States Righters, and Peace Democrats and War Democrats and Protectionists and Free-Traders, and Manufacturers, and Labor Reformers, and Woman's Righters, and Spiritualists and Internationals, and Catholics and the United Sons of America into our party: but I think it could have been done, as well as to have caught a part of the negro vote. But it is too late now. The Woman's Righters, and Spiritual-

ists, and "Reformers" of all grades and ideas are against us: and even the Democrats won't vote the ticket.[17]

Some people became Liberal Republicans because they disliked Grant's undignified style, his crude manners and inept conduct,[18] while others opposed Grant's support of carpetbag governments and favored a more conciliatory attitude toward the South. Still others objected to Grant's slow action toward civil-service reform or (for various and not necessarily consistent reasons) dissented from Grant's currency and trade policies.[19] This incoherence of the party toward currency and trade questions has been called its greatest weakness. The Liberal Republicans "held almost every economic view then in vogue. Some were conservative and some radical, some for a high tariff, some for a low, some were gold men and some were greenbackers. To complicate the confusion, a number of professional politicians who were on the outs with Grant and had no interest in reform attached themselves to the party. With its only unifying factor being opposition to Grant, the Liberal movement lacked a basis for either success or permanence."[20]

The other major reason for the failure of the Liberal Republicans was their nomination of Horace Greeley for the presidency in 1872. The Liberals might have nominated Charles Francis Adams or some respected leader,[21] but the managers of Greeley's campaign, to the dismay of Schurz and other reformers, were able to start a stampede at the convention for Greeley.[22] Greeley's nomination was a tragic mistake. It was said of Greeley that "his odd appearance—throat whiskers framing a pink face; white overcoat and socks—his peculiar mannerisms, his advocacy of queer causes, gave him the reputation, fatal in politics, of being an eccentric. The object of cruel abuse in the campaign of 1872, he wondered if he was running for the Presidency or the penitentiary."[23] Given this portrait of the nominee, it is not difficult to understand why the *Times* called its opponents not liberals, but Greeleyites.

The party bolters of 1872 designated themselves as liberal partly because the leaders, either by intuition or conscious plan, grasped the advantage of being called liberal and partly because their original leaders identified themselves to some extent with the Liberal party in England. However favorable this symbol was, it was not powerful enough to compensate for a completely disunited party led by a vilified eccentric. Given its inadequate program and leader, the movement and its identifying symbol never became viable. Grant won by a landslide over the Liberal Republicans; Greeley carried only two southern states and four border states, and against Grant's 186 electoral votes he won only 62.[24] For many years afterward no important group would choose to call itself liberal, because this label had become identified with such a losing cause.

Progressivism and the New Republic

The next important moment in the history of liberalism in the United States occurred in 1916. In order to understand the significance of this moment, we should review the relevant background.

Walter Weyl, Herbert Croly, and Walter Lippmann were three intellectual fathers of the Progressive movement. They were very close to Theodore Roosevelt.[25] When Roosevelt ran for the presidency on the Bull Moose ticket in 1912, Weyl, Croly, and Lippmann were his loyal supporters. After his defeat, Roosevelt accepted the failure of the third-party movement, saying, "The fight is over. We are beaten. There is only one thing to do and that is to go back to the Republican party."[26] But Weyl, Croly, and Lippmann, as they came together to form the *New Republic*, felt that the new party could become permanent.[27] Croly, for example, wrote to Roosevelt, "Now that the first skirmish is over and the long campaign begun, I feel that the moment has arrived to consider the question of organizing the party on a permanent, democratic, and self-supporting basis."[28]

The new magazine editors at first extolled Roosevelt's virtues, but it became clear that Roosevelt would not be won over to the *New Republic*'s ideas. Yet the editors were not enamored of the incumbent president, Woodrow Wilson, either. "Their progressive philosophy demanded a strong leader to promote democracy and nationalism. But the *New Republic* had no leader."[29]

For the election of 1916 the *New Republic* decided at first to support the Republican nominee, Charles Evans Hughes,[30] and defended him against the charge that a justice of the Supreme Court should not run for president. But the magazine wanted a strong leader, and it was not long before its editors criticized Hughes's mildness. Their dissatisfaction with Hughes increased by the end of July.[31]

Meanwhile, Colonel Edward House and other supporters of Wilson saw the advantage of winning Progressive votes.[32] Although by 1916 the *New Republic's* circulation was only about 24,000, it was quite influential, and its contributors and supporters included Charles Beard, Randolph Bourne, John Dewey, Felix Frankfurter, Learned Hand, and George Santayana. "The *New Republic* had already a name for itself among intellectuals, and upon the intellectuals the independent and progressive vote in part depended," says Charles Forcey.[33] Particularly on the East Coast, the magazine was an element to consider.

Responding to this influence, Wilson began to adopt the policies of Roosevelt's New Nationalism. The first sign of this shift in policy was Wilson's nomination of Louis Brandeis to the Supreme Court on January 28, which the *New Republic* heartily approved. Then Wilson supported the Hollis-Bulkley farm credits bill; the *New Republic* had favored this measure since 1914. By the autumn of 1916, Wilson's Democratic Congress had, in fact, enacted into law virtually every important plank of the New Nationalism of 1912, and by August the *New Republic* had clearly shifted to Wilson's support.[34]

In July, while the *New Republic* still had some misgivings, the magazine stated: "What *liberals* need to obtain from Mr. Wilson is some assurance . . . that his later preference for a governing government will not prove to be as fugitive as his earlier preference for doctrinaire freedom." Charles Forcey, an astute student of this period, comments: "The use of the word 'liberals' in this instance is the first the author has noted in the *New Republic's* pages."[35] He has also observed:

> Croly, Weyl, and Lippmann . . . had betrayed a subtle shift in their own thought even as they recited their misgivings. They were now talking about "liberal," not as always before, "progressives." The shift in terms showed

the strength of the lure of Wilson's power, but, to the subsequent confusion of American political thought, it also marked the piracy of a word that belonged rightfully to the Jeffersonians. By August, when Hughes made his acceptance speech, the editors could without blush complain that the Republican had "not yet justified the faith of liberals."

"Liberals" now suited the *New Republic* men better than "progressives," because the old name was redolent enough of the Bull Moose to embarrass any rally around a new leader.[36]

Forcey argues that since the Jeffersonians believed in a limited central government, it is only proper to call them liberal, but "liberal" could "rightfully" belong to the Jeffersonians only if words cannot change their meaning. But words do change their meaning. As Justice Holmes acknowledged in 1918: "A word is not a crystal, transparent and unchanged, it is the skin of a living thought and may vary greatly in color and content according to the circumstances and the time in which it is used."[37]

Around the turn of the century in the United States, "liberalism" probably implied Manchester economics. It is because of this implication that one author has argued that Americans had to use the term "progressive" to describe their reform movement.[38] In England, by 1916, Hobhouse's definition of the new liberalism had clearly triumphed. To those Americans such as Weyl, Croly, and Lippmann who were in touch with British politics, it was not strange to use the word "liberal" by 1916, because that term no longer needed to have Manchester connotations. Because the new tag was appropriate, and because the old term, "progressive," was inappropriate due to its close association with their former ally Roosevelt, it was natural for the *New Republic* editors to begin to use the new symbol. "Liberal" was a good and unencumbered word.

President Wilson, of course, continued to refer to himself as "progressive." However, Wilson and his associates (including, presumably, Franklin D. Roosevelt) did read the *New Republic*. By 1932 the columns of that magazine, but not yet the general press, fully embraced the terminology of "liberal" and "conservative," giving those words much the meaning they later possessed under the New Deal and in succeeding years.[39]

Liberalism in the United States, 1919–1932

Although the liberal symbol was not yet commonly used in political debate by the general press or by the great majority of the people before 1932, certain left-wing political organizations began to adopt the new term with increasing frequency. Why these organizations—which were very small, generally very local in scope, and very uninfluential—chose to identify themselves with liberalism is a question easier to ask than to answer. Perhaps they identified themselves with Continental or British liberals, or they may have been influenced by the *New Republic*'s use of the term. Perhaps all of these groups, which sought to increase their own liberty, called themselves liberal because they associated liberalism with liberty and freedom from restraint.

The first time that the *New York Times* reported a political group using the name "liberal" was in 1921. The *Times* announced that the president of the Liberal League of Negro Americans urged blacks in New York to arm themselves.[40] The insignificance of this league is indicated by the fact that this first short announcement of its activities was also the last. The next year the *Times* informed the voters, in two short notices, that the Massachusetts Liberal Republican League opposed the reelection of Senator Lodge.[41] The effectiveness of this organization is reflected in the *Times* observation: "This move is of great surprise, but is not expected to hurt Senator Lodge, even though the League has conducted a vigorous campaign."[42] After November 1922, we hear no more of this league.

Later the *Times* reported that yet another league, the Liberal League of Mid-West Colleges, was planning a conference of students and workers "to take steps for the abolition of war."[43] This group also was insignificant, for if the conference was ever held, it was not newsworthy enough to be reported. (And if it was held, it quite obviously failed.)

In 1924 the *Times* indicated that a Liberal Immigration League existed and that it advocated immigration from Europe "without regard to number and independent of our immigrant population."[44] Three years later the Liberal Civic League of Massachusetts was briefly able to win news coverage when it presented a petition to the Massachusetts legislature suggesting repeal of the Prohibition amendment.[45]

None of these leagues was significant, either individually or as a group, but it is significant that left-wing organizations chose to place the term "liberal" in their titles. It indicated that "liberal" no longer had connotations of Manchester economics, not only for the *New Republic* editors, but also for various reform groups.

While all of these leagues were quite local in scope, in the years before 1932 there were two major attempts to form national liberal parties. In terms of political activity, both were utter failures, although each reflected pockets of discontent with the political life in the 1920s and possibly made easier the realignment of political forces during the 1930s.

The first group that tried to form a Liberal party called themselves the Forty-eighters. In 1919 this group formed the Committee of Forty-eight, which was to organize a Liberal party in order "to avert on one hand the extremes of radicalism and on the other the extremes of reaction."[46] The brief history of the Forty-eighters' attempts to form a new party reads something like a comic opera.[47] By the middle of 1920, Non-Partisan League delegates from South Dakota broke from the Forty-eighters in favor of the Labor party convention, soon after the Forty-eighters quit the Farmer-Labor party.[48] Finally, while Robert LaFollette was considering whether he would accept the nomination for president on the Liberal party ticket, there was a third bolt in the party when Forty-eighters who opposed LaFollette's nomination formed their own Liberal party.[49] This anti-LaFollette convention held in Chicago drew only about fifty delegates, and they expected that they would name no presidential ticket. Lester Barlow, the leader of the World War Veterans who was not allowed to make an address to the convention, threatened to call still another convention. He charged: "I have never seen so

many nuts collected in Chicago as during the past few days." [50]
This third-party movement failed completely, and in 1924, when
LaFollette did run as a third-party candidate, he ran under the
Progressive label. [51]

In 1930 the *Times* reported that a second group was attempting
to form a national liberal party. Samuel H. Church, president of
the Carnegie Institute, announced the "creation of a new political
party, to be known as the Liberal Party, whose chief aim would
be to divorce the government from every form of religious dicta-
tion and seeking the dissolution of every society which aims
to subordinate any part of the citizenship because of race or
creed." [52] Church added that he was very much against Prohibition and that the "noble experiment" should be repealed.
Church claimed that his proposal for a Liberal party was a great
success:

> A new party—the Liberal Party—had been proposed,
> and its reasons for being had been clearly demonstrated.
> The men whose names had appeared in the discussion
> received hundreds of telegrams and thousands of letters,
> from every State in the Union, and virtually from every
> town in every State. "We want the Liberal Party," they said.
> "We need the Liberal Party. The soul has gone out of the
> old parties. Liberty is dead. America is perishing. Go on!
> The country is with you. God bless you!" These were the
> things which the people were saying from their deepest
> emotions. [53]

The *Times*, in a more somber mood, reported the cold recep-
tion that Church received. A Pennsylvania representative, who
was leader of the wet bloc in Congress and who warned that the
Republican party would disappear if it continued to support
Prohibition, still opposed a Liberal party, and Senator Borah
commented, "Third parties, where do they go?" [54]

The *Times* proposed two main reasons for the easy rejection of
this third-party movement, one focused on history and the other,
interestingly enough, on labels. First, reasoned the *Times*, politicians remembered that Teddy Roosevelt's and Robert LaFollette's
Progressive parties had failed; and second, politicians realized
that "their policies are better advanced by adhering to the old

party names and party organizations, even when these politicians are opposed to everything that their party stands for."[55]

Although liberalism did not yet have an important role in American political debate, these two third-party attempts did prepare the way for (and help cloud the meaning of) the new symbol. The first group, the Forty-eighters, by calling themselves liberal, contributed to the confusion of that term. The original Forty-eighters were a splinter group of expelled German liberals who came to the United States and continued their polemics against Catholic groups here.[56] The new Forty-eighters were apparently their intellectual descendants. The greater part of their membership, their secretary said, was from the business and professional classes,[57] and they favored, among other things, the reduction of the president's powers in foreign relations, reduction of the Supreme Court's power to declare laws unconstitutional, public ownership of the transportation system, and "literal restoration of the constitutional rights of free press, freedom of speech, and public assemblage."[58]

The meaning read into the word "liberal" by the actions of the Forty-eighters was essentially different from the liberalism of Church's party. Church's liberals were not intellectual descendants of expelled Germans but generally were Republican businessmen. Church himself was an active Republican,[59] and Pierre DuPont, chairman of the executive committee of the Association Against the Prohibition Amendment, endorsed Church's proposal for a new Liberal party.[60] Among the approximately one hundred men at the meeting held in New York City during which the proposal was made to create the Liberal party, there were "captains of industry, railroad presidents, college teachers, steamship officials, bankers, [and] merchants."[61] This Liberal party platform, very unlike that of the Forty-eighters', placed much emphasis on opposition to Prohibition, blue laws, and "those egotistical bigots who leave their cheerless pulpits and go to Washington and the State capitals to demand laws for controlling the conduct of their fellow men."[62] When one group of Forty-eighters and another group of anti-Prohibition businessmen laid claim to the favorable symbol of liberalism, the net effect was to help introduce and help obscure the meaning of the word.

One might expect that if "liberal" is a favorable political symbol, and that if politicians realize the advantage of owning that symbol, then some people would object to the attempted expropriation of it by the organizations just discussed. The discussion that one would expect to ensue would, of course, be on a small scale, since these organizations were small and somewhat less than significant. In fact, such a small debate did actually occur.

One of the foremost advocates of his type of liberalism was Dr. Nicholas Murray Butler, president of Columbia University during the 1920s. It may not be easy to summarize his political philosophy in one paragraph, but I think it would be fair to argue that many of Butler's beliefs would be considered conservative today. Rexford Tugwell has called him a "paragon of reaction," and a student under Murray's presidency reminisced:

> The president of our university had forfeited our serious attention when he annually affirmed his opposition to the child-labor amendment. Moreover, we were always being reminded of his harshness toward such distinguished faculty members as Beard, Dana and Cattell when they refused to join the academic goose step in World War I. . . .
>
> He did have an extraordinary capacity for saying things that invited derision. "Child labor does not exist in the United States. . . . This is the undoubted fact despite the quite irrelevant statistics marshalled in opposition to it," the papers quoted him as saying one day during state hearings on the child-labor amendment. On another day we woke up to read that he had said, "Much of the talk of maldistribution of wealth is sheer invention . . . mischievously devised by radicals" and on still another he observed that "capitalism is a debating term invented by Karl Marx." [63]

But Butler considered himself to be a very good example of a liberal. In 1923 he passionately felt that "liberalism is in eclipse in the United States and throughout the greater part of the world," and complained that because liberalism was dying, it was possible for its enemies to struggle for its name: "There are those who by striving to lay hands on the name of liberal and to apply it to illiberal and anti-liberal doctrines of every sort have already brought it into contempt, so that the followers of the great liberals in the history of the English-speaking peoples are confused and ashamed. . . . Not a few liberals are discouraged, and what wonder! They see their name stolen by their critics and their enemies because of its noble associations." [64]

Although Butler never really made clear what he meant by liberalism, he did say that liberals are by necessity progressives and cannot be reactionary because the powers and satisfaction of liberty never stand still. A progressive, he also added, is *not* one who fixes prices by law, puts government chains on commerce and industry, attempts to control the personal habits and conduct of men, or by law relieves any group of citizens from the responsibility of paying taxes. [65]

Two years later, in a symposium, "Liberalism: The Gospel of the Open Mind," Butler no longer declared that liberals must be progressive; liberals may occasionally be conservative, or even radical, depending on changing conditions, he argued. The essence of liberalism now was not progressivism but "the holding fast to [the liberal's] faith and liberty," since the "true liberal is a believer in liberty, whether that liberty be intellectual, civic, political, economic, or religious." [66]

Dr. E. Martin Hopkins, president of Dartmouth College, seemed to agree with Butler that left-wing elements were stealing the word "liberal." In his opening address to the two thousand students of Dartmouth in 1923 he warned: "We have . . . at the present time . . . extremists who style themselves 'liberal,' with a capital 'L,' . . . [who] exploit in their interests the field of liberal thought. This professionalized group, arrogating to itself all virtue and good intent and denying these qualities to all others . . . is doing more to breed suspicion of *true liberalism* than is being done or could be done by all available forms of reaction if combined in militant array" (emphasis added). [67] Hopkins, like Butler, feared that the label of liberalism was being stolen, but, unlike Butler's liberalism, Hopkins's was narrowly defined as tolerance. It had significantly fewer economic implications.

William Allen White was a far different person from Butler. As early as 1917, White argued for railroad nationalization, federal old-age pensions, and public operation of the natural resources "along socialistic lines." [68] Speaking at the same symposium at which Butler spoke, White did not noticeably differ in rhetoric from Butler's vague brand of liberalism, saying, "I am a liberal. I have always felt that God gave us a mind not to close but to open to truth."[69] There is no evidence that White ever claimed in the 1920s that radical elements were stealing the title of liberal.

Alfred E. Smith had an even more amorphous concept of liberalism. At the same symposium with Butler and White, Smith told his audience that he believed in "the fostering of good-will and tolerance." He also added optimistically, "Civilization is in itself progressive and it cannot go forward without the liberals who lead the way. It is an old accepted truism that the cranks of one generation are the leaders of the next."[70]

Several of these intellectuals thought that liberalism was being exploited by left-wing groups, and although all of these men had generally vague definitions of liberalism, they all thought that liberalism was good and that they were liberals. In the entire decade of the twenties there were apparently only two major figures who explicitly attacked liberalism. On the extreme right, Mussolini denounced liberalism and parliamentarianism,[71] and on the far left, the Socialist Norman Thomas, after differentiating liberalism as a doctrine of tolerance and liberalism as the doctrine of laissez faire, claimed that laissez-faire liberalism had "definitely collapsed." He added, "Much that passes for liberalism or progressivism, especially in the Middle West, was really retrogressive."[72]

In the few instances in which liberalism was discussed in the 1920s, all respectable public opinion leaders declared themselves to be liberal. The propitiousness of the liberal symbol was probably increased by the fact that in this period of normalcy the only significant people who attacked liberalism were a Fascist and a Socialist. Both Mussolini and Thomas meant different things by liberalism, of course, but they both attacked the same label.

This debate over the proper use of "liberalism" was very restrained, and most readers of the newspapers probably took little notice of it, though the *Times* did write several editorials on the subject. These editorials give the general impression of frustrated resignation. The *Times* objected to the more left-wing elements of society who proclaimed themselves to be liberal. Writing in an era in which people did not realize that many of these apparently extreme ideas would someday become common-place, the *Times* argued that these left-wing elements would have been more appropriately labeled "radical" or "red." However, while objecting to the expropriation of "liberal" by the radicals, the editorials seem resigned to new uses for the old label. While the *Times* argued that the new liberals should be called radicals, it appeared to accept calling them liberals.

In 1922, for example, the *Times* attacked those "self-styled liberals" who cried, "'Liberalism' is in decay." These liberals did not blame their doctrine, as they should have, said the newspaper; instead, they claimed that the "fault lies with a world turned suddenly narrow and reactionary." The editorial recommended:

> A manly candor would compel the self-styled liberals to confess the tyranny of trade-union domination, the destructive blindness of "industrial democracy," and seek new light, new leading. The lines of hopeful experiment are striking out in many directions. Employè or "company" unions contain the seed of truly representative institutions in industry. . . . While attacking the most modern problems of human welfare, the new liberalism is true to the spirit of the Fathers—most of all in the fact that it looks steadily, courageously forward. But the professional liberals will have nothing to do with it. They stand apart, with minds open at both ends, wailing from time to time that liberalism is in decay.[73]

Although the editorial objected to these self-styled liberals, and although it considered company-union liberalism to be a better liberalism, the editorial did continue to call its opponents liberals.

In 1923, an editorial referred to the formation of a Liberal League and called its preliminary declaration of principles "highly respectable." These principles included the halting of the "tendency of Government interference in every domain of life," the maintenance of individualism, and the assertion of the right and duty of the people's representatives to vote according to their judgment and conviction. The editorial approved of the principles but called them conservative. "Persons who call themselves 'Liberals' at Washington and in the several states try to quicken instead of halting Government interference in every domain of life. Government by majorities, if not outworn, is a conservative principle." The editorial concluded: "The only trouble with the Liberal League is its name. It might better frankly call itself the Conservative League."[74] In another editorial, when advocating the "waiting for proof of the new before abandoning the old," the *Times* bluntly called such scientific skepticism "conservative."[75]

In 1924 the *Times* sadly argued that since the World War, "there has . . . been a change in names and labels. One such notable change has been the expropriation of the time-honored word 'Liberal.'" Since the armistice, "in the newspaper headlines it was merely a question of space whether something was Liberal, Radical or Red." The editorial concluded with a hope that eventually "the Radical-Red school of thought might be compelled to hand back the word 'Liberal' to its original owners."[76] The *Times* objected but also resigned itself to the expropriation of that "time-honored word."

Six years later the *Times* repeated almost exactly this editorial of 1924. Once again the editorial argued that since the war a great amount of violence had been done to the "historic name" of liberalism. Once again the editorial pointed out that for "several years after the Armistice it seemed to be entirely a matter of headline space whether the police took cognizance of a Liberal meeting, a Radical meeting or a Red meeting."[77] That practically the same argument that had been presented in 1924 was presented again in 1930 shows the *Times*'s continual recognition of and resignation to the expropriation of the liberal symbol by a number of left-wing elements.

In the 1920s Dr. Nicholas Murray Butler would never have surrendered the title "liberal" without a fight; yet the *Times*, perhaps reflecting and molding the views of its readers, was more easily resigned to the new meaning of liberalism. Perhaps, unlike a skilled politician such as Butler, the *Times* did not realize the importance of liberalism and the increased significance that was being attached to the label.

Since liberal was a vague but favorable symbol, and since this symbol had not yet been widely used, it appears possible that Herbert Hoover, given the national platform of an incumbent president, might have been able to win designation as a liberal before Roosevelt had a chance to introduce and popularize the symbol for a wide audience. In fact, before 1932 Hoover did claim that he was a liberal. In 1928, for example, he attacked—in the name of liberalism—Governor Smith's advocacy of government intervention: "Every step of bureaucratizing of the business of our country poisons the very roots of liberalism—that is, political equality, free speech, free assembly, free press, and equality of opportunity."[78]

However, before the New Deal, although Hoover occasionally referred to himself as liberal, he did not make any intensive effort to *capture* the label—that is, to popularize it and give it meaning so that it referred solely to his philosophy. What little evidence there is during this period indicates that Hoover both recognized and accepted the fact that many elements that he considered illiberal were calling themselves liberal. Hoover argued:

> It is these human rights and the success of government which has maintained them that have stimulated the initiative and effort in each individual, the sum of which has been the gigantic achievement of the nation. . . .
>
> Never had these principles and ideals been assembled elsewhere and combined in government. This is the *American system*.
>
> We have lived and breathed it. We have seldom tried even to name it. Perhaps we might well abandon efforts to define it—for things of the spirit can be little defined. Some have called it liberalism, but that term has become corrupted by political use. . . .
>
> Ours is a system unique with America—an expression of the spirit and environment of our people—it is just American.[79]

When the newspapers reported the speech, liberalism was, of course, unmentioned. A typical article could say only that

Hoover supported the American system, something that could not be defined.[80]

Perhaps Hoover did not yet realize the advantage of being able to apply the liberal label solely to his own philosophy. Another possible, and I think very likely, explanation for Hoover's apparent resignation at this time is that "liberal," as explained in Chapter 1, was not yet an important political tag. The label existed, and intellectuals and major politicians were aware of it and occasionally used it; however, the term had not yet become an important symbol of common speech. Hence it would have been unusual for Hoover to have placed great emphasis on it.

We have seen the circumstances under which the influential *New Republic* looked to the British Liberal party and introduced the term "liberal" into American politics. After this introduction, several left-wing or protesting organizations adopted the term, while people we would today call conservative objected to this new American use of "liberal." The *New York Times* editorials and President Hoover objected—but not strongly—to what they thought was a misuse of a time-honored word. All of these activities occurred, of course, on a very small scale and were the preparation for the much more widespread discussion of liberalism in the 1930s.

The Great Debate: 1932–1940

The Antagonists: Hoover and Roosevelt

Herbert Hoover was truly a great Progressive. Though a registered Republican, he sent a campaign contribution to Theodore Roosevelt and publicly supported his Bull Moose party in 1912.[1] During World War I Hoover began to earn much respect from people such as Louis Brandeis and Woodrow Wilson—first because of his aid to Americans stranded in Belgium, and then because of his administration of relief in that country. By 1918, Hoover had made such a national reputation as an effective war food administrator that his name had become a household word. In 1920 Brandeis and the *New Republic* began a Hoover-for-President campaign.[2] At this time Franklin D. Roosevelt wrote of Hoover: "He is certainly a wonder, and I wish that we could make him President of the United States. There could be no better one."[3] During the 1920s, when the country endured the administrations of Warren G. Harding and Calvin Coolidge, and when progressivism had disappeared from the White House and no longer had a majority in Congress, Hoover was considered one of the progressive champions of the national government.[4]

Yet Herbert Hoover had a tragic flaw. Hoover the great Progressive, the great engineer, and the great humanitarian was also the great dogmatist. He had in his mind a very clear idea of what progressivism was; to venture one step beyond that idea was to him absolutely un-American. Hoover would use federal governmental power in a negative manner—for example, traditional trust-busting—but would be reluctant to use such government power in a positive way—for example, to feed people.[5] In 1931 he declared that desperately poor people should be fed but that this care was a voluntary and local responsibility, for "if we start appropriations of this character we have not only impaired something infinitely valuable in the life of the American people but have struck at the roots of self-government."[6]

Hoover practiced what he preached. During World War I he had tried to run Wilson's Food Administration as far as possible on a voluntary basis.[7] Later, while secretary of commerce, he induced Harding to persuade the steel companies to grant an eight-hour day. Notice that the steel companies granted the eight-hour day; Hoover did not press for a law to regulate hours but urged voluntary regulation.[8] Later, as secretary of commerce under Coolidge, Hoover established some two thousand voluntary trade associations to aid small businesses—associations that could in theory "establish codes of ethics, standardize production, establish efficiency, and make substantial savings." In practice many members of the voluntary associations did not abide by their rules, as Franklin D. Roosevelt, head of the American Construction Council, soon discovered.[9]

Rexford Tugwell has succinctly summarized Hoover's personality: "Hoover was not an engineer at all in any factual sense, but a man of principle. . . . There was almost no distinction, in his mind, between federal relief for the unemployed, for instance, and Communism."[10]

While Hoover was dogmatic, Roosevelt was flexible. For example, although Roosevelt believed in government economy so strongly that he objected, while governor of New York, to even such small expenses as per diem compensation to the Nassau County mosquito extermination commission, and while he enthusiastically accepted the Democratic platform's economy plank in 1932,[11] he also could argue in that year, "I believe that we are at the threshold of a fundamental change in popular economic thought. . . . The country needs and, unless I mistake its temper, the country demands bold, persistent experimentation. . . . Above all, try something."[12]

Both Hoover and Roosevelt imitated the methods that the Progressives had used to direct the economy in World War I, but Roosevelt was not bound by Hoover's dogmas. Both Hoover and Roosevelt were ready "to label these measures as voluntary—

but in contrast to Hoover, . . . [Roosevelt] was ready to put into them in fact the teeth of compulsion. Voluntary methods had not worked very well."[13]

Roosevelt and Hoover each represented a major school of thought in the 1930s. Hoover and his followers objected strongly to Roosevelt's violation of the dogma that it is wrong for government to act positively.[14] While Hoover was certainly no Herbert Spencer, yet had the same fanatical zeal of a Spencer, he and his followers argued that Roosevelt's program was a precursor to socialism, or even worse was socialism itself, masked under the name of liberalism.

Rexford Tugwell observed that both Hoover and Roosevelt "regarded themselves as liberal capitalists, even if the Roosevelt definition would have included planning and direction. They differed on a question of instrumentalism—what was end and what was means and what could therefore properly be manipulated and what had to be regarded as untouchable. If this seems narrow ground for so epic a struggle it is nevertheless the ground on which it is taking place. It was—and is—that kind of struggle. And it is by no means yet settled."[15] In this chapter we shall analyze a part of the struggle that for a great majority of people is settled; that is, we shall examine Hoover's attempt to "unmask" Roosevelt as a false liberal.

Roosevelt's Need for a Symbol

In order for President Roosevelt to engage effectively in "bold, persistent experimentation," he had to capture a favorable symbol that would help to ward off expected attacks labeling his programs as "communistic" or "socialistic." Tugwell pointed out that, in order to win support in their struggle against change, reactionaries have to impute "to their opponents either rascality or non-conformance so that their own moral superiority could be urged in indignant language." This Roosevelt adviser then elaborated: "But, political machines being what they were, rascality was usually more available to reformers. . . . Non-conformity was the great resource of the

other side. What heretics were to the Middle Ages, 'reds' became to the twentieth century. This was an effective competing
objective. . . . The danger that he might be tagged 'Red' with all
that follows from such labeling, made Mr. Roosevelt cautious
about stating any objective except the 'preservation of capitalism,' a renunciation in which other progressive leaders also
felt forced to join."[16] FDR's political sense was keen enough to
realize that in the United States the label "Red," or even "socialist," is the sign of opprobrium.

"Socialist" is such a reproachful term here because of what
Louis Hartz calls our liberal tradition.[17] Because there has never
been feudalism in America, no aristocracy has developed with
an ideology to support its privileges, and therefore, no Far Left
could develop in opposition. This Far Left, where it does develop, has to form a counterideology (in order to justify its position) that rests on fundamentals contradictory to those beliefs of
the aristocracy. In the United States both Toryism and socialism,
and the labels that represent these philosophies, are unnatural
and foreign. Applying America's liberal tradition to the New
Deal, Hartz observes: "Had Roosevelt said, 'we have to go
beyond Locke but not as far as Marx,' and had he translated
Locke into 'Americanism,' which was of course its meaning
here, he would have alienated many of his followers from him.
. . . 'Americanism' was gospel, the very thing which made socialism alien, and any conscious transgression of it . . . was
highly unpalatable."[18] Roosevelt therefore needed an appropriate symbol so that he would be able to justify his new policies in
terms other than socialism.

It also would have been advantageous for Roosevelt to capture
a favorable, "forward-looking" word as a means of counteracting
the wealth of conservative symbols that for years were being built
into society. Both Rexford Tugwell and Thurmond Arnold have
listed several "sacred words" that had been captured by the conservatives. "Individualism," Tugwell and Arnold believed, was
used by some as a justification for not caring for the indigent;
"independence" was taken to prevent union membership; and
"freedom and liberty" were twisted by some to mean that corporations were individuals that had to be protected at all costs.

"Liberty of contract" meant that it was unconstitutional for Congress to enact a minimum wage for women and children working in Washington, D.C.[19]

Roosevelt had to counteract these old sacred words partly by redefining them and partly by introducing a new symbol. He had to understand the functions of symbols in order, in Thurmond Arnold's words, to "make men as enthusiastic about sensible things as they have been in the past about mad and destructive enterprises." It was not enough for the government to aid the indigent, encourage union membership, or support unemployment insurance—measures that could be justified on pragmatic or humanitarian grounds. Roosevelt also had to justify these measures on a symbolic level. As Arnold realized, "the humanitarian values which [many of Roosevelt's measures] represent, and which prevent us from abandoning them, . . . [should be] tied up with . . . [a] theological structure which gives us peace and certainty for the future."[20]

The third major reason why it was particularly important for Roosevelt to be identified with a term of favorable connotations was that he could use that label to win electoral support outside of the Democratic party. Roosevelt needed to introduce a political label that would allow voters to think in terms other than Republican or Democrat. By associating his policies with a word such as "liberal," instead of "Democratic," a sympathetic Republican could more easily justify his vote for FDR because he could mentally say to himself, "I am for Roosevelt, not because he is a Democrat, but because he is a liberal." Roosevelt used the liberal label to operate as cross-pressure against the significant factor of party identification.

Roosevelt must have been acutely aware that his party was in a distinct minority position. In 1920 the Democratic presidential ticket, with Roosevelt running as vice-president, had won only 34.1 percent of the total vote. Four years later this figure dropped even lower, to 28.8 percent, and in 1928 the Democrats, although raising their total presidential vote, were still soundly defeated and polled only 40.8 percent.[21] While all politicians generally appeal to voters outside their own party, it was essential for Roosevelt to win many Republican votes.

While Roosevelt was governor of New York, he explicitly ordered Samuel Rosenman, his speechwriter, never to attack Republicans or even the Republican party, because this would alienate the many Republicans whose votes he needed. Roosevelt, who continued this policy throughout his career, explained to Rosenman: "There are thousands of people who call themselves Republicans who think as you and I do about government. They are enrolled as Republicans because their families have been Republicans for generations. . . . So never attack the Republicans or the Republican party, only the Republican *leaders*. Then any Republican voter who hears it will say to himself: 'Well, he doesn't mean me, I don't believe in the things Machold and McGinnies and Knight and the other reactionaries up in Albany believe in either.'" [22]

This policy of Roosevelt's assured that he would not automatically *repel* Republican votes; yet, to win elections he had to *attract* Republicans. The logical extension of FDR's policy, then, would be to introduce a term that could identify his ideas on government and still not be so attached to the Democratic party that it could not be used to attract Republicans. Roosevelt understood this and stated explicitly:

> I have always believed, and I have frequently stated, that my own party can succeed at the polls so long as it continues to be the party of militant liberalism. . . . There is a vast number of independent voters who are unwilling to become affiliated with either party, but whose social and political outlook is definitely liberal, and whose votes have been cast for liberal candidates. On the other hand, millions of enrolled Republican voters—affiliated under the conservative Republican leadership for one reason or another—have nevertheless consistently voted for the type of government and candidates who appear under the liberal banner. [23]

President Roosevelt realized that in order to ward off more effectively the attacks that he was a "Red," to negate conservative symbols, to make men and women enthusiastic about his programs, and to widen his basis of electoral support, he had to capture a favorable political label.

Inappropriate Symbols for
Roosevelt's Program

There were several possible terms with which it would have been unfavorable for Roosevelt to identify. He could have called himself a Socialist, but such a foreign tag would have alienated many followers. "Democratic" was a possible label, but emphasis on this word would have made it more difficult for him to attract much Republican support. "Social Democratic" had the disadvantage of both worlds, for it sounded "faintly un-American" and also would not draw Republicans.[24]

Roosevelt could have relied solely on the phrase "New Deal" to identify his program, and in fact this term—to which Roosevelt attached no special significance when he introduced it in his acceptance speech to the Democratic convention—did become the hallmark of his program, even though it was the press, and not FDR's premeditation, that endowed the phrase with importance.[25] The great advantage of "New Deal" was that, since it had no historical definition, Roosevelt's actions would automatically breathe into this pliable term its entire meaning. Yet this advantage was also a disadvantage; because the word was born with no meaning of its own, either good or bad, it was less useful as a means of counteracting conservative symbols and winning support from those who did not want to be so closely tied to his administration. For these reasons, it was to FDR's advantage not to rely solely on the tag "New Deal" but also to introduce a symbol that had inherently favorable connotations, even though such a word might be more difficult to capture.

No doubt a label that was a prime contender was "progressive"; in fact, Rexford Tugwell, an adviser to Roosevelt, preferred this term because of his "not liking the English 'Liberal.'"[26] However, the great disadvantage of identifying with progressivism was that the term was not an empty enough word to be in the public domain. That is, the word was closely identified with the Progressive movement led by many Republicans such as Theodore Roosevelt and Robert LaFollette. Even Herbert Hoover was well known as the Great Progressive. Also,

Roosevelt wanted to experiment, but "the economics of American progressives was anything but experimental."[27] Rather than attempt to change the meaning of a well-used word and risk the possibility of association with Hoover, it was much more logical for Roosevelt to try to capture a term that was favorable but not well used and that did not have any publicly agreed-upon definition.

Roosevelt Chooses a Symbol

Roosevelt instinctively chose to capture "liberal" and identify his programs with that term. We will never know for certain exactly why he chose that particular label, but we can make some reasonable guesses. Tugwell recalled once talking to Roosevelt about the origin of his use of "liberal," but Roosevelt did not answer him, though "he laughed and asked if it mattered."[28] Roosevelt probably did not answer because he had not consciously chosen the liberal symbol, just as he had not consciously chosen the label "New Deal." Rather, as Raymond Moley believes, "the use of the term at that time was not arrived at with any premeditation or precision." Moley adds, "I speak with some authority on this because I did assemble and direct the group upon which Roosevelt depended for the development of campaign policies in 1932 and I was very close to him in 1933 when the programs were being formulated and presented to Congress."[29]

It was not particularly surprising for Roosevelt to identify with the word "liberal," for he must have been reading the *New Republic* and would have understood that magazine's use of "liberal" and "conservative." Further, he was probably aware that several reformist elements of society had been using the term.

Roosevelt had been using the term before the New Deal, but he had not made it his own. As early as 1919, at a banquet of the Democratic National Committee, he spoke of "conservatism, special privilege, partisanship, destruction on the one hand—liberalism, common-sense idealism, progress, on the other."[30] Yet he had not popularized this liberal-conservative dichotomy, for as late as 1931 we can find Roosevelt comparing and contrasting conservative politicians or ideas to Progressive (rather than liberal) politicians or ideas.[31] Apparently it was not until 1932 that Roosevelt began to popularize the liberal-conservative terminology.

Just as it was Roosevelt's style instinctively to understand the need for a symbol that would allow him to engage in bold and persistent experimentation, he probably also instinctively understood what I argued in Chapter 2—that "liberal" was an inherently favorable term for a politician to adopt, that this label had laudatory implications, and that it captured the drift of modern history.

Probably the main reason why FDR chose "liberal" was that he identified with the philosophy of the British Liberal party. We have seen how both the Liberal Republicans of 1872 and the *New Republic* of 1916 looked to England when they searched for a political label. Roosevelt very likely followed this tradition. Dr. Moley states that "perhaps it [liberal] was [used] because we felt that the philosophy we were suggesting was rather close to that of the Liberal Party in England—the party of Gladstone and Lloyd George."[32]

We have already seen how the Campbell-Bannerman and Asquith governments in England provided models for some New Deal legislation and that Keynes, during the time of the New Deal, perceived the Liberal party to be the middle ground for controlling and directing economic forces. Roosevelt and many of his advisers also saw their philosophy as being the middle way; they had the same perceptions as Keynes.[33]

Roosevelt wanted the middle way, and he made clear that to him "the middle course is, and I quote what I have said before, 'just a little bit left of center.'"[34] Like the Liberals of England, every member of the Brain Trust rejected laissez faire, trust-busting, or socialism. Instead they favored various forms of business-government cooperation and believed that no element in society should hold a preponderant power.[35]

If we could imagine Roosevelt in England, we could more easily appreciate how similar his philosophy was to that of the British Liberals. Louis Hartz asks,

What would he have said had the American Socialist party been the English Labor party . . . ? Obviously under such circumstances Roosevelt would be speaking very strange language indeed. He would be defending private property, he would be assailing too much "bureaucracy," he would be criticizing the utopian mood in politics. After pleading for the TVA and the SEC and the HOLC, he would proceed to qualify his faith in the state by an attack on the larger radicalism which faced him to the left. In other words, instead of being "radical," he would be half radical and half conservative, which is precisely the unfortunate position that the Liberal reformers of Europe were compelled to occupy. Instead of enlisting the vigorous passions of youth, he might easily be described as a tired man who could not make up his mind; a liberal who tried to break with Adam Smith but could not really do so.[36]

I am not contending that Roosevelt was directly influenced by Keynes's perceptions of liberalism, for these two men really did not even understand each other.[37] Yet both Keynes and Roosevelt were free of a dogmatic belief that government cannot act in a positive manner, and both perceived themselves as seeking a solution to the Great Depression, a solution that they saw as middle-of-the-road. Hence Moley's supposition—that in 1932 the New Dealers felt their philosophy to be close to that of the Liberal party in England and therefore called themselves liberals— is logical and reasonable.

Instinctively, for FDR had good instincts, Roosevelt had seen the need for an advantageous label and had chosen it; yet this decision did not end the story of the term "liberal." Rexford Tugwell was at least one Brain Truster who appreciated the problem: "In the transition from an old to a new progressivism . . . great care had to be used. . . . To be progressive was respectable enough; but the enemy's game was to prove that individual progressives were 'radicals.' Any wine therefore had to be put carefully into the old bottles and the size of the letters on the label had to be increased in proportion to the dilution of the contents."[38] The struggle to capture the word "liberal" had begun.

The Beginnings of the Debate:
1932–1933

From the very beginning of the New Deal, Roosevelt adopted the liberal tag. When accepting the Democratic party's nomination for president, for example, he called that party "the bearer of liberalism and of progress."[39] In his second message to Congress, on March 10, 1933, in a speech written by Moley,[40] FDR justified his request for powers to slash $500 million from the budget by warning, "too often in recent history, liberal governments have been wrecked on the rocks of loose fiscal policy."[41]

Americans were not really concerned with what Roosevelt was calling himself at this time. This was the period, until June 15, 1933, in which the country was experiencing the frenzy and motion of the Hundred Days. The president could do no wrong. In May 1933, Anne O'Hare McCormick reported the mood of America: "Something far more positive than acquiescence vests the President with the authority of a dictator. This authority is a free gift, a sort of unanimous power of attorney. . . . Industry, commerce, finance, labor, farmer and householder, state and city—virtually abdicate in his favor."[42] Some of the president's measures, even deflationary ones such as budget cuts, were not questioned but were accepted as "surgical measures for chronic tumors in the political and financial systems."[43]

On the whole, as Arthur M. Schlesinger, Jr., says, "the feeling of movement was irresistible," and there were few signs of protest.[44] The *Des Moines Register* was one of the rare harbingers of later dissent. "The world today," its editorial argued, "does not know what true liberalism as applied to conditions of now really is." It continued: "In this country we are in the midst of the dizziest period as to that question that we have ever known. This much is certainly true, that it is the Hoover type of mind that is still standing in these times for the individualistic dogma that was the fundamental of original liberalism, and that it is the Roosevelt type of mind that is insisting on far-reaching measures which are the reverse of individualism. Yet practically everybody, without dissent, rightly or wrongly, looks on Hoover as the conservative and on Roosevelt as the liberal."[45]

Actually, not everyone did look on Roosevelt as the liberal; we find that for the first time the issue of what liberalism really meant became important enough that a reader of the *New York Times* was prompted to write a letter to the editor concerning the proper definition of liberalism. Roosevelt had wanted bold and persistent experimentation, but it was in the name of liberalism itself that the reader objected, categorically asserting that "the liberal is not an experimenter."[46] For the most part, however, the issue of what Roosevelt was doing to that grand old word "liberal" was being ignored, and even one major corporate business magazine—probably not understanding what Roosevelt meant or would mean by "liberalism"—proudly announced to its employees: "If you are lacking in confidence in our President's understanding of the many problems that must be solved in staying this drastic liquidation and bringing about definite and wholesome improvement, read a book just published, *Looking Forward*, by Franklin D. Roosevelt. The cover sheet carries the following: 'We are about to enter upon a new period of liberalism and of sane reform in the United States. . . . As President of the United States I shall do my utmost.'"[47]

Willard Kiplinger, who wrote an influential business newsletter, argued that it was not until March 1, 1934, that business reaction against Roosevelt became significant.[48] That this thunder on the right did not appear until 1934 was of great advantage to the New Deal, for it furnished a period of grace in which Roosevelt's programs could be identified with liberalism unhampered by any serious challenge to the New Deal's power to define this term.

The First Round of Debate: The Election of 1934

Since 1934 was an election year, the attack by the Right greatly increased in an attempt to convince the American people that they (the Right) were the true liberals. It was in this year that a group of very conservative Democrats and some members of big business such as Alfred P. Sloan—"finding the Republican party an inadequate vehicle for the expression of their indignation"—established the Liberty League to save the country by launching a direct attack on the New Deal. The Liberty Leaguers would have preferred a new McKinley to a New Deal, and they probably would have preferred a new Mark Hanna to either.[49] (Mark Hanna, the prominent nineteenth-century captain of industry, Republican National Party chairman, and political kingmaker, typified the turn-of-the-century marriage between the Republican party and big business.)

I am not really concerned with the activities of this group, because the league was so extremist and represented such a small part of public opinion that even Herbert Hoover refused to join it.[50] Moreover, its main emphasis in political debate, the symbol upon which it focused, was not liberalism but the American Constitution. As one member of the league's executive committee, speaking of the Constitution, contended: "I do not believe that many issues could command more support or evoke more enthusiasm among our people [than the Constitution]. . . . There is a mighty—though vague—affection for it. The people, I believe, need merely to be led and instructed."[51]

A more important, and more interesting, attack came from the less extreme conservatives, led by Hoover. Hoover's *The Challenge to Liberty* appeared in 1934 and, says Arthur M. Schlesinger, Jr., "provided a comprehensive statement of the conservative position."[52] Hoover claimed:

> Liberalism holds that man is master of the state, not the servant; that the sole purpose of the government is to nurture and assure these liberties. All others insist that Liberty is not a God-given right; that the state is the master of the man. . . .
>
> On other occasions I have commented upon the perversion and assumption of the term "Liberalism" by the theories of every ilk—whether National Regimentation, Fascism, Socialism, Communism, or what not. I have pointed out that these philosophies are the very negation of American Liberalism.

And I may add a word to that group of people in and out of government who are playing with Socialist fire without expecting it really to burn. The penetration of Socialist methods even to a partial degree will demoralize the economic system, the legislative bodies, and in fact the whole system of ordered Liberty. . . . In the United States the reaction from such chaos will not be more Socialism but will be toward Fascism.[53]

Hoover and his followers carried this argument to the people, shouting that Roosevelt's policies were socialistic.

What was really liberalism? This question was actively discussed on a popular level by a great number of people. We saw in the previous chapter that in 1924 and 1930 two *Times* editorials argued that the time-honored word "liberal" had been expropriated after the war. For the third time the newspaper repeated this argument, claiming, "The good old pre-war word, liberal, standing for progress with order, was captured by a much tougher crew after the armistice, so that Liberal, Radical and Red became interchangeable."[54] For the first time the editorial provoked a response from the readership: "One reads that 'the good old prewar word Liberal has been captured by a much tougher crew.' Is this not an ungenerous characterization of such men as Herbert Hoover and John W. Davis—about the only citizens nowadays who are willing to make public proclamation of their liberalism?"[55]

Another disturbed reader quickly replied. His answer is worth quoting in its entirety:

By what right and on what basis does Elmer Davis [the author of the previous letter] speak of Herbert Hoover and John W. Davis as "Liberals"? There is nothing in the known policies and actions of these men that will in any sense justify the title.

The word "liberal" has been taken in vain by a great many persons since the World War but surely it is vainest of all to apply it to men whose points of view are out of accord with that characteristic of liberal-mindedness.

The liberal attitude is certainly that of belief in the improvability of human situations by means of specific legislation without being scared off by foolish and irrelevant cries such as "regimentation" and "socialistic." The liberal is further willing to let the other fellow shoot off his mouth with his political opinions.[56]

Professor John Dewey, during a symposium entitled "The Future of Liberalism," added that those who oppose basic reforms are "blind and stubborn reactionaries."[57] Yet the *Times* sarcastically charged that "a 'Liberal' administration is one that comes down with the cash. A 'liberal' is a patriot who wants all he can get from 'liberal' Uncle Sam, turning his pockets and those of the taxpayers inside out."[58] The debate was on.

Since Roosevelt and Hoover and their followers were all claiming to be liberals, there must have been great confusion. Samuel Beer hypothesizes that to end this semantic problem the New Deal liberals called their opponents "conservatives."[59] That Dewey was trying to label the Hoover school of thought as reactionary and that the opponents of FDR complained that Hoover was being unjustly tagged as a conservative does support Beer's reasoning. However, since Hoover did not readily accept the appellation of "conservative," and since the United States did not have a Liberal party that had the right to define "liberal," the confusion continued—as we shall see—for some time.

An article that appeared in the *New York Times Magazine* during this period probably reflected quite accurately the general populace's confused notion of liberalism in the early 1930s. It could hardly have been written today. It was titled "Liberalism Faces a World Challenge," and its author was P. W. Wilson.[60]

Wilson immediately presents the problem: America is confronted by a "sharp issue. . . . It is an issue that has been stated in the plainest terms. According to Secretary Wallace, the nation has to decide whether it will or will not surrender certain liberties of the people to economic necessity. In the Old World, Liberalism has been largely abandoned. Has Liberalism become impossible in the New World?"

Wilson then notes that there had never been so "many organized expressions of what was understood to be Liberalism" as there were in 1934. In Geneva there was the League of Nations, and "even in Asia we find parliaments." The number of schools had multiplied. This was the era of opportunity; yet somehow "over much of the civilized world the very Liberalism which promoted our civilization should now be stamped out by the police as an evil thing."

Liberalism apparently had triumphed and yet had not triumphed. Attempting to explain this paradox, Wilson says: "Clearly we need to rid our minds of confusion and ask ourselves what Liberalism really means." He claims that "Liberalism is a charter of liberty for the individual" that applies to all governments of whatever form. This charter guarantees that there are certain matters, such as those of conscience, "in which the free citizen has the right and duty to be his own master." Wilson seems to be arguing that liberalism means tolerance.

Then, while describing what wonders this doctrine of liberalism achieved in the past, Wilson gives us another definition: "It was Liberalism that put through the great schemes of old age pensions and national insurance against unemployment, sickness and maternity. It was Liberalism that threw open the universities of Oxford and Cambridge to all classes and races, that carried the first and fundamental scheme of national education." Liberalism now seems to mean state welfare activities. As if to give justification to this interpretation, Wilson later says, "No grievance need arise if the State extends its functions by undertaking responsibility in an elaborated community for the regular supply of necessities like gas, water and electricity. It is not a grievance that the State should supervise railways and banks in so far as such supervision is necessary to safeguard the interest of the public."

Liberalism now means much more than tolerance. Yet Wilson contradicts himself when he explains what is the liberal economic philosophy:

> In economics the teaching of Liberals has been no less clear. They have accepted the dictum of Adam Smith that the wealth of nations is interdependent; that commerce between nations is of general benefit to all and special benefits to each. . . .
>
> Deficits on budgets, fluctuations of currencies, repudiation of financial obligations—all these evidences of chaos

would have been unthinkable to the great financiers in Britain: Pitt, Peel, Gladstone and the rest, who, whatever may have been their party label, applied Liberal ideas to the administration of the Exchequer.

In short, liberalism is tolerance and individualism, but it is also a state administering welfare and regulating the business in the public interest—and doing all of this under the rules of classical economics.

While presenting his definitions of liberalism, Wilson also classified several people as liberal. One might guess that such a list would lessen the confusion over the meaning of liberalism.

In fact, the opposite effect is achieved. Wilson classifies John Stuart Mill as a liberal, and somehow Thomas Carlyle—who attacked Mill, liberalism, and the greatest happiness principle— also qualifies as a liberal. We discover that Abraham Lincoln "became a symbol [of liberalism] for all mankind," and that Thomas Jefferson was "perhaps the greatest Liberal of them all." Walt Whitman, Charles Dickens, and several others are liberals, too. What Wilson says in effect is that anyone who is well remembered was a liberal. His notion of who liberals are is as confused as his notion of what liberalism is.

The American people on the whole were probably just as confused about the proper meaning of liberalism as was Wilson. Roosevelt sensed their confusion and tried to persuade them that positive government is not dictatorship. Minimizing the differences with American tradition that the New Deal represented, Roosevelt pointed out that "the conservative British press has told us with pardonable irony that much of our New Deal program is only an attempt to catch up with English reforms that go back ten years or more."

Responding to Hoover's challenge, Roosevelt replied in kind: "My friends, I still believe in ideals. I am not for a return to that definition of liberty under which for many years a free people were being gradually regimented into the service of the privileged few. I prefer and I am sure you prefer that broader definition of liberty under which we are moving forward to greater freedom, to greater security for the average man than he has ever known before in the history of America." [61]

I am certain that the great majority of Americans were still confused; they would not have been able to agree on what true liberalism actually was. Yet Roosevelt appeared to be taking positive action to fight the depression, and it was clear that freedom had not yet been subverted. "Most people simply could not accept the portrait of the American government as a totalitarian dictatorship," says Arthur M. Schlesinger, Jr.[62] In the midterm elections, the Democrats did not lose seats, which would have been normal in an off-year. Instead they gained ten seats each in the House and Senate.[63]

The debate was not yet over, but the New Dealers had won the first round.

The Second Round: 1935–1936

From the very beginning of the New Deal, Roosevelt's policies differed from Hoover's and from those of the other Progressives. Tugwell saw the New Deal policies as so dissimilar that he concluded, "Looking back from the beginning of the New Deal in 1933, the radical movements preceding it seem to have been pretty mild, usually—deserving the name radical only by courtesy, certainly not by comparison."[64] After the 1934 election, which inaugurated what was to be called the Second New Deal, it became even clearer to Americans that Roosevelt's policies were transcending much American tradition. He was now beginning to give more emphasis to reform not only to achieve economic recovery but also for its own sake. This Second New Deal was far to the left of the First Hundred Days, and it enabled Roosevelt to become the "champion of the new political coalition of farmers, laborers, and millions of underprivileged."[65]

Although from the very beginning Roosevelt was doing something different in American politics, his divergence from past policies became much more apparent to the articulate public in general during this Second New Deal, for Roosevelt was responding with new proposals to a more class-oriented electorate. It was in this period, specifically in the 1935 session of Congress, says Raymond Moley, that Roosevelt powerfully urged "social security, aimed essentially at urban wage-earners; the Holding Company Act, which undermined the strength of the big power companies; and the Wagner Act, which put government squarely behind the labor movement. Roosevelt's major messages and speeches took on a flavor of strong opposition to business interests."[66]

Tugwell has observed that Roosevelt's "departure from tradition followed practical necessities for some time before it became apparent that the design being created would have seemed strange to Wilson or the predecessor Roosevelt."[67] Arthur Krock, a discerning witness of this time, was one of the first to sense the new design and to realize that the New Deal was shifting gears. Commenting on Roosevelt's first appearance before Congress in 1935, Krock noted: "In his opening message this week to the first Congress elected on a referendum of the New Deal—a Congress overwhelmingly pledged to support him and his *maturing policies*—the President chartered a definite course for what *may in time be known as twentieth-century American liberalism*" (emphasis added).[68] Krock predicted that Roosevelt's new policies might capture the title of "liberal," and added that, in Washington at least, the great majority of public thought favored the president "not apparently or solely as Democrats or New Dealers . . . but as subscribers to his permanent character of liberalism. Responsible legislators and administrators in the mass seemed to find in it no socialism."

Although Washington agreed that the new policies should be called liberal, the rest of the country was not as convinced, for Krock admitted: "Liberalism has never been defined to the complete satisfaction of any liberal." However, Krock tried to present the "correct" definition:

> The Britannica gives what it considers the best definition, and, if the President's message is examined in the light of this description, it will be seen to reflect many of its principles:
>
>> Liberalism is a belief in the value of human personality, and a conviction that the source of progress lies in the free exercise of individual energy; it produces an eagerness to emancipate all individuals or groups so that they

may freely exercise their powers, so far as this can be done without injury to others; and it therefore involves a readiness to use the power of the State for the purposes of creating the conditions within which individual energy can thrive, of preventing all abuses of power, of affording to every citizen the means of acquiring mastery of his own capacities, and of establishing a real equality of opportunity for all. These aims are compatible with a very active policy of social reorganization, involving a great enlargement of the functions of the State. They are not compatible with socialism, which, strictly interpreted, would banish free individual initiative and responsibility from the economic sphere.

While the comment can be made that *one advanced section of liberalism would oppose the limitations on individual acquisition and power* which the President pledged himself to impose, another liberal group has always held that the State must, in varying degree, protect the many weak from the full development of the economic and political strength of the strong. This was the President's thesis and he fortified it with more detail than he has ever given before [emphasis added].[69]

Krock, like Roosevelt, used the definition of liberalism as a justification of the New Deal. Although he admitted that there were some who called themselves liberal and yet allowed unlimited individual acquisition and power, he dismissed them. They refused to be dismissed, however, and for the 1936 election they made a desperate effort to seize the label "liberal."

The Republican platform for the 1936 election, declaring that "America was in peril," dedicated the party to "the preservation of . . . political liberty." Old-age annuities and unemployment insurance were condemned as "unworkable," and Republicans "pledged themselves to maintain the Constitution and to preserve free enterprise."[70] The presidential nominee who had to face Roosevelt was Alfred Landon, governor of Kansas, who had bolted the party in 1912 to support the Bull Moose Progressives. But although Landon was the nominee, Hoover had hardly disappeared from the scene. It "was ex-President Hoover who in speech and in writing attacked the procedures of the Democrats and formulated again and again the Republican case," says Denis W. Brogan. [71]

Representing the anti–New Deal position, Hoover told the Republican party that it had had "the greatest responsibility" since the days of Lincoln, for it had had to uphold "the standard of American principle." There is "one issue that is never outworn," he argued. "That is human liberty. The party must become the true liberal party of America." Hoover was specific in his attack. "Today the term liberalism is claimed by every sect that would limit human freedom and stagnate the human soul, whether they be Fascists, Socialists or New Dealers." The New Deal, he said, was a "false liberalism" that regimented men and extended bureaucracy. He went on, "Liberty and opportunity do not flourish on a deficit of three billions a year." [72]

In another speech, in which he was introduced as "a real liberalist, not the anarchistic, communistic, socialistic type that we have now," Hoover warned that the New Deal's ideas "are dipped from cauldrons of European fascism or socialism." In this speech Hoover suddenly changed topics and devoted most of the remainder of his time to a discussion of the symbol "liberalism." He complained:

> We hear much as to who is a Tory, a reactionary, a conservative, a liberal or a radical. . . . You can elect yourself to any one of these groups if you say it often enough. If you do not like anybody you can consign him to the one which is most hated by your listener.
>
> Taking a compound of definitions coming out of Washington, the impression would be that . . . the liberals have the exclusive right to define the opinions of others. . . .
>
> As a matter of serious fact, these terms have been used mostly for camouflage and for political assassination. The natural choice of youth is toward true liberalism. . . .
>
> It is false liberalism that interprets itself into dictation by government. [73]

Roosevelt clearly understood that the Republican leaders had decided to "base their campaign upon the charge that the New Deal was an 'alien' form of philosophy," so FDR decided to assault this issue frontally. Therefore, in his very first speech of the campaign he assured the people: "I have not sought, I do not seek, I repudiate the support of any advocate of communism or of any other alien 'ism' which would by fair means or foul change our American democracy. That is my position. It has always been my position. It always will be my position." [74]

Roosevelt's supporters joined with him in defending the New Deal in terms of the symbol "liberalism." John Dewey, for example, wrote a historical summary of liberalism, contending that liberalism had two strains: humanitarianism and laissez faire. In the United States, he argued, "liberalism has been identified largely with the ideal of the use of governmental agencies to remedy evils from which the less-fortunate classes suffer." He charged Hoover and the Liberty League with "identifying the meaning of liberty and rugged individualism with the maintenance of the system under which they prospered." Dewey concluded, as had Roosevelt, that "laissez-faire liberalism is played out," but the remedy for a better society is not violence but rather liberalism, which is not afraid to use state action. [75] Even the *New York Times*, which earlier had been lamenting the loss of that word, now published an editorial that differentiated between liberals and Communists, even though it said that many liberals look "forward ultimately to a classless society, democratically controlled, in which collectivism coexists with full liberty for the individual." [76]

Although Hoover continually insisted that he was the true liberal, the 1936 election offered the first instances of some Hoover-like liberals who began to call themselves conservatives. In replying to Dewey's defense of liberalism, one reader insisted—as we would expect—that "true liberals" are "vehemently opposed to government control of daily affairs of citizens" and that no new legislation is needed. However, he also added that "true liberalism and conservatism merge." [77]

We are told in another article that "your true liberal may be toward many ideas and ideals most conservative, but he . . . presses on. With him there are imperishable values in history and experience which no age can afford to ignore." [78] Except for diehards such as Hoover, some conservatives in 1936 were beginning to abandon the liberal symbol and claim the conservative label.

In 1936 the people had to decide if Roosevelt's policies meant greater liberty or tyranny. The design of his policies was then much clearer than in 1934. Roosevelt, of course, won every state but Maine and Vermont. Unlike the 1932 election, in which people of all classes deserted the Republican banner, the New Deal in 1936 won "each successively lower-income group . . . in larger proportions."[79]

We saw in Chapter 2 how the advanced Whigs captured the tag "liberal" and were able to make it viable and lasting because their name change was accompanied by a fundamental change in policies and the introduction of class politics. For somewhat similar reasons, although the dichotomies of America are more moderate than those of England, the New Deal won the battle for the word "liberal."

As it became clearer that the New Deal was going beyond American tradition, it became logical to apply a new name to those new policies. The new name was "liberal" and not "Socialist," partly because Roosevelt's political instinct rejected the Socialist label and instructed him to insist that he was a liberal, operating under a definition of liberty that allowed positive government action, and partly because the Hoover school of thought was insisting that socialism meant regimentation and tyranny. Since the great majority of people had not felt any great loss of freedom, they would not, by Hoover's definition, equate socialism with the New Deal.

Before 1932 most people had not been calling Hoover liberal, for he was a Progressive. Since his policies had not changed, it was unreasonable for people to give him the new label. By 1936 most people probably also agreed that Hoover was not liberal. Raymond Moley summarized the process by which "liberal" came to identify Roosevelt's proposals. It was in the Second New Deal, he said, that "the trade name 'Democratic' was kept, but the substance of the party's heritage . . . [underwent] a metamorphosis. And with the change there came into use the word 'liberal' to describe an ideology based on the enlargement of the power of the Federal government and an abundance of welfare programs."[80]

The debate to capture the liberal symbol logically should have ended with the 1936 election; in the next section we shall see why it actually continued.

The Third Round:
The Court-Packing Plan

The 1936 election results were fairly convincing evidence that the great majority of people accepted FDR's new policies and the new name he applied to them. Conservative Republicans should have realized the futility of their insistence that they (the conservatives) were the true liberals. Indeed, the debate might have ended except for Roosevelt's attempt to pack the Supreme Court.

Because of the Court's many anti–New Deal judicial decisions, and after FDR's tremendous vote of confidence, the president became determined to alter the Supreme Court.[81] On February 5, 1937, he proposed that Congress give a Supreme Court justice or lower federal court judge past the age of seventy six months in which to retire. If the judge or justice failed to retire within the appointed time, he could not be removed from the bench, because the Constitution grants lifetime tenure. But under FDR's proposal, the president would be able to appoint an additional judge or justice, who—in theory—would be younger and more able to handle the judicial work load. The maximum number of additional judges who could be appointed was fifty, and the total maximum membership to which the Supreme Court could be expanded would be fifteen, a maximum that would in fact be reached, since six justices were then over seventy years old. Roosevelt would then have up to six new appointments on the High Court.[82] Though Roosevelt presented the plan as a means of getting new blood in the judiciary, the opposition and the general public found this argument disingenuous and labeled the proposal with the pejorative epithet, "Court-packing plan."

From the very beginning this plan ran into tremendous opposition from many congressmen, a great majority of the newspapers, and, of course, the American Bar Association, for the Supreme Court was an important symbol in itself, a symbol of liberty in a world that was seeing Hitler's rise to power. The general public, who just a short time before had given the New Deal a great margin of victory at the polls, also joined vigorously in the opposition to the plan, for "through the years, and despite increasing evidence that judicial interpretations and not Fundamental Law shackled the power to govern, the American people had come to regard the Court as the symbol of their freedom." [83]

Most people know the end of this story: Roosevelt did not pack the Court, and the Court stopped trying to repeal the New Deal. [84] The significance of the episode in the liberal debate is that because of this Court plan, conservatives could join with liberals in attacking the proposal as illiberal. This was not the major ground for the attack on the Court plan, but it was one basis. Although liberalism was hardly the decisive factor in the Court fight, the fight was a major factor in the debate over liberalism.

In the Senate, for example, the leader of the opposition to Roosevelt's proposal was no conservative but the liberal Senator Burton K. Wheeler, who justified his opposition in terms of liberalism. "A liberal cause was never won by stacking a deck of cards, by stuffing a ballot box or packing a Court." [85] Since even liberals were attacking Roosevelt in the name of liberalism, conservatives could make the same attack and once again claim that they themselves were the true liberals.

Looking at the pages of the *New York Times* for this period, we find that by far the greatest number of articles discussing liberalism appear to be in response to Roosevelt's Court proposal. For example, the former secretary of state, Bainbridge Colby, "warned against misuse of the term liberal." After presenting the usual incantations such as, "Liberalism is the cooperation of voluntary association, toryism is the cooperation of coercion," he became more specific and instructed that liberalism "involves absolute independence of the judiciary. Toryism is the integration of power, and such a coercive regime seems the very antithesis of liberalism." [86] His implications must have been clear.

Later the *Times* printed a long editorial titled, "Liberalism and Tempo." [87] The beginning of this editorial presented general attacks on the new liberals: "Liberals may defend a Klansman on the Supreme Court [Hugo Black for a time had been a member of the KKK] because he is sound on the Administration's economic program. The new Liberal will condone labor violence on the ground that employers have long practiced violence in strikes, and it is now our turn." That "fine old word 'liberal,' with a small 'l,'" said the editorial, has been "sometimes thrown out of the window, by the Liberal with a capital 'L.'" While liberals believed in moderation, "the new Liberal is in a hurry."

Given this introduction, the *Times* editorial then launched into a strong attack, in the name of liberalism, on the Court-packing proposal. Roosevelt's New Deal reforms were good, the article said, but the true liberals would rather accept the delay of these reforms than accept Roosevelt's plan for the Court. Because of the Court, America might have lagged in social justice, but the lag has not been a denial. Concluding, the *Times* warned: "How dangerous anti-democratic speed may become has been amply demonstrated in those countries where despotism presides over tempo."

This editorial, perhaps because it reflected contemporary public opinion so well, was greeted with a tremendous number of responses. One reader warned that "the so-called new liberals" are moving in a "blind rush." Another reader, agreeing with the Supreme Court that many New Deal programs were "in violation of the accepted principles of government of the people," added that the Court proposal was a product of "self-conceived 'liberal' thought" that at the very least established a precedent that provided "a grave fear of future danger." Another called the editorial an excellent "example of liberal thinking," and yet another observed: "Jefferson, truly liberal if ever man was, after advising a correspondent in a letter of July 12, 1816, that although Constitutions should be amended when necessary, added: 'I am certainly not an advocate for frequent and untried changes in laws and Constitutions.'"[88]

Of course, not all the responses to the editorial were favorable. Many of those who approved of the Court plan justified it in the name of liberalism. Speaking of the same editorial, one reader charged, "It is the old story of the laissez-faire school denouncing the fighters for social progress as radicals and revolutionaries." Another reasoned, "Liberalism was gradualist when the world was gradualist. Can it afford to take one step at a time when progress, or at any rate change, on so many other fronts is made by leaps and lurches? Isn't liberalism forced to quicken its tempo if it is to survive at all?" Another simply suggested, "For the editorial 'Liberalism and Tempo' you should go straight to bottomless perdition."[89]

Since much of the public—liberals and conservatives—opposed the Court plan because it was not thought to be in the spirit of liberalism, the debate over what should be called liberal, and if Roosevelt should really be called a liberal, was artificially extended, even though Roosevelt had already logically captured the term. However, although the Court proposal extended the debate over "liberal," it also helped prepare the way for the acceptance of the label "conservative" by the conservatives. Because the Court plan to some extent discredited the New Deal in the minds of many people, by association the Court plan also tended to discredit New Deal liberalism. Since New Deal liberalism became suspect, the word "liberalism" became a little tarnished. It therefore became easier for conservatives to accept another label that in their eyes was not tainted.

The Purge of 1938

In 1938 the president was stunned by reversals in Congress, just two years after his overwhelming reelection. What most exasperated the New Dealers was their belief that the country was more liberal than the Congress, and that "many Democrats had won office on Roosevelt's popularity only to knife him as soon as the returns were counted." A council of liberals was formed to study the possibility of purging conservatives from the party.[90]

On June 24, impatient with conservatives of his own party and irritated by the election victory of Guy Gillette, a staunch anti–New Deal Senator from Iowa, Roosevelt began the purge. Against his opponents he hurled a new (and yet old) symbol, when he charged that they were "copperheads": "Never in our lifetime has such a concerted campaign of defeatism been thrown at the heads of the President and Senators as in the case of this seventy-fifth Congress. Never before have we had so many copperheads—and you will remember that it was the copperheads who, in the days of the War between the States, tried their best to make Lincoln and his Congress give up the fight, let the nation remain split in two and return to peace—peace at any price."

Roosevelt then argued that, not as president, but as head of the Democratic party, charged with carrying out its liberal platform, he had the right to speak in Democratic primaries between conservatives or liberals or in cases "involving a clear misuse of my own name." Liberals, Roosevelt argued, recognize "that the new conditions throughout the world call for new remedies," while conservatives "do not recognize the need to step in and take action to meet these new problems."[91]

Later Roosevelt went even further in his declaration and announced that he would prefer liberal Republicans to conservatives of his own party, and that he would continue to campaign for the election of liberals in national and state politics, regardless of their party affiliations.[92]

The manner in which symbols were used in the purge illustrate both FDR's awareness of their importance and his opponents' increasing recognition of the power of words. After Roosevelt had tried to label all conservatives as "copperheads," the *Herald Tribune*, a Republican paper, responded with the charge that Roosevelt was pinning a new tag on his critics to "tar them with utterly undeserved prejudice." Significantly, the paper then queried, "Did the advocate of this technique, Mr. Thurmond Arnold, suggest the use of 'Copperhead,' we wonder?"[93] Since Arnold had written his own study of symbols, *The Symbols of Government*, in 1935, and had been appointed assistant attorney general in March 1938,[94] the *Tribune* had good reason to wonder.

Rather than argue who were the "true copperheads," FDR's conservative opponents, who by now had had several years of experience in battling symbols, called Roosevelt's actions a "purge." As William Leuchtenberg has pointed out, since the word "purge" quickly became the generic term for Roosevelt's actions, "the President [had] placed himself on what seemed the

wrong side of a 'moral' question." The word "summoned up images of the bloody extermination of Roehm and other Nazi leaders by Hitler in 1934 . . . [and] as the Czech crisis built toward
the showdown at Munich, it was easy to represent Roosevelt's
move with the same unquenchable appetite for power that possessed the European dictators." [95] Although FDR objected to the
tag and argued that the word "purge" was used "by those who
were opposed to liberalism" in order "to misrepresent my conduct . . . ," the label stuck. [96]

Roosevelt campaigned for the election of liberals, but on the
whole the purge was considered a failure. Of all the races in
which he intervened, only in New York was the anti–New Deal
candidate defeated. [97]

The purge failed for many reasons. For one, the New Deal's
prestige was falling because of the Court-packing plan, union
problems in 1937, and the Roosevelt recession in the fall of
1937. [98] The purge itself was also badly handled and "executed in
an amateurish and only half-committed fashion." [99] Probably another main reason for the failure was that Roosevelt assumed
that the country was much more ideological than it actually was.
Though New Deal politics were more class-oriented than previous American politics, and although "liberal" was a useful label
to justify actions and win support across party lines, Americans
still lived with the liberal tradition, where politics were not
solely class politics and ideological feelings were mild. As
William E. Leuchtenburg has observed:

> Roosevelt had hoped that, by distinguishing between lib-
> eral and conservative representatives, he could win popular
> support for the creation of a liberal Democratic party. Un-
> happily, ideological issues that seemed clear in Washington
> blurred in South Carolina. . . . Liberalism and conservatism
> became confused in an encounter which pitched the might
> of the federal machine against the State House crowd, a con-
> test in which each candidate sought to outdo the other in
> whipping up race hatred. In the end, Smith [South Caro-
> lina's anti–New Deal candidate] won by splitting the vote of
> the millhands. "It takes a long, long time," the President
> commented wearily, "to bring the past up to the present." [100]

The unsuccessful purge is useful not only to show the limits of the power of the symbol "liberal" but also because it gives evidence of a trend that began in 1936 but was briefly interrupted in 1937; that is, in 1938, often in response to the purge, we read that even more conservatives than in 1936 were calling themselves conservative. Some conservatives, to be sure, still insisted that they were properly called liberal. One Republican senatorial candidate claimed that true liberalism was "summed up in the sentence that 'Those people are governed best who are governed least,'" and the Republican national chairman seconded this observation when he declared, "The true Republicans running for Congress this year are liberals and most of the Democrats seeking re-election are not." [101]

To a very great extent, however, conservatives began accepting, even embracing, the label of "conservative" and argued that conservatism was better than liberalism. For the first time we read that a man like Senator Glass, for example, defined a liberal as "a man who is willing to spend somebody else's money." As we might expect, a conservative is defined as "a man with good sense." Elliott Roosevelt, who on some occasions had been sharply critical of his father's programs, "defined the liberal as one who was ready to 'try anything once' and the conservative as one who 'stops, looks and listens before he leaps.'" One reader attacked liberals by defining "a 'liberal' in Congress . . . [as] one who is always liberal in spending the taxpayer's money," while another defended conservatives by writing that it was on "the conservative American philosophy" that the foundation of this nation was built. [102]

More and more conservatives seemed no longer to be afraid of calling themselves conservatives and attacking liberals. Even the *Des Moines Register*, which was, as we saw earlier, one of the first newspapers to complain that it was improper to call FDR a liberal, now happily accepted the new terminology and hoped that America would enter into "another sober-conservative period." One New York group, which was so reactionary that it thought Dewey would turn the state to the Communists, started a new party, and they did not hesitate to call it the Conservative party. [103]

Just as 1936 marked the logical end of the debate, 1938 marked the beginning of the end of the actual debate. After this point there was a precipitous decline in the number of news articles on liberalism—not because people stopped using the term, but because it became less newsworthy. People were beginning to stop debating about it, and more and more conservatives were accepting the designation of conservative.[104]

The End of Public Debate: 1939–1940

After 1938 the New Deal's interest turned much more to foreign affairs than previously. Roosevelt was becoming more concerned with the world crisis; as some historians have noted, "he had not abandoned the New Deal, but it was in abeyance."[105] As the president and the American people began to think more of possible war, they talked less about the term "liberal." In 1939 a headline announced that various Democratic officials, including Paul McNutt, the Social Security administrator, and Aubrey Williams, the National Youth administrator, predicted that liberalism would be the 1940 election issue; in fact, the issue was national defense.[106]

The issue of the proper ownership of liberalism was not completely settled, though, for few issues are ever completely settled. A poll taken in 1939 showed that "four out of ten voters have little idea of how to define a 'liberal,' a 'conservative,' and a 'radical,' in spite of President Roosevelt's emphasis on the distinction."[107] If we focus on the more articulate and well-read public, however, on those who were more politically aware and probably had some idea of what "liberal" meant, we should look at the opinions of the 60 percent who could define the labels. Only 1 percent of those who could give some definition of the terms and who had opinions thought of Roosevelt as a conservative; 55 percent felt that he was a liberal, and 41 percent called him a radical. (The poll indicated that most of those who called him a radical were Republicans.) Only 5 percent of the people who could give some definition of the terms and who had opinions thought Hoover was a liberal; somehow, 3 percent said he was a radical, although by far the great majority (92 percent) called him a conservative.

In short, not only did rumors of war significantly reduce the discussion of liberalism, but more and more conservatives were accepting the label "conservative," and articulate people in general agreed that Roosevelt was the liberal and Hoover was not. Roosevelt had won a symbol that proved to be much more viable than "New Deal."

5 Roosevelt and a National Liberal Party

Several students of the Roosevelt era have argued that FDR desired to realign American politics so that all the conservatives would be in one party and all the liberals in the other.[1] The disastrous failure of the purge of 1938 clearly showed that this realignment would not take place. "That man Roosevelt" seemed to have learned his lesson after this debacle. For example, in 1940 he refused a request to speak out on behalf of Senator Harry Truman, who was opposed in the Missouri primary. Stephen Early, the White House secretary, explained to Truman that it was the president's "'invariable practice' to take no part in primary campaigns. 'The President must stand aloof,' said Early, 'regardless of any personal preference he might have.'"[2]

Yet Samuel Rosenman contends that as late as 1944 Roosevelt actually believed that "from the liberals of both parties Willkie and I together can form a new, really liberal party in America."[3] Rosenman explains that after Dewey won the nomination in the 1944 convention, because of conservative Republican opposition to Willkie, Willkie then discussed with Governor Pinchot the possibility of the liberals in each party joining together and expelling all conservatives. Pinchot reported to Roosevelt, who told Rosenman that he agreed with Willkie's idea "one hundred percent and the time is now—right after the election. We ought to have two real parties—one liberal and one conservative."

FDR then asked Rosenman to contact Willkie and discuss the proposed new liberal party. However, since many Republican liberals had been urging Willkie to endorse Roosevelt, and since Willkie had chosen to remain silent, the president warned Rosenman to explain to Willkie that the meeting would have nothing to do with the 1944 election. Therefore Willkie would not think the meeting was an effort or subterfuge to win his support.

At the secret meeting Rosenman told Willkie, "The President learned in 1938, the hard way, that he cannot beat them [the conservatives] in their own districts. He is now ready to form a new grouping, leaving them out of the new liberal party. You see, you both are thinking along the same lines. He wants to team up [with] you." Willkie agreed with Rosenman and said that he thought that the work should begin immediately after the 1944 election. However, since Willkie died before the election and FDR died shortly after, the "herculean task that these two political leaders had thought of undertaking" was never even started.

That is Rosenman's argument; but the facts that he gives allow a very different interpretation—that is, that Roosevelt permitted Willkie to believe he was willing to start a liberal party in order to win, or imply that he had won, Willkie's support for the 1944 election.[4] This 1944 episode with Willkie was really Roosevelt's last great use of the concept of liberal to bridge the gap caused by party labels and to win, or at least appear to win, the endorsement of a prominent Republican. Even if Roosevelt had not secured Willkie's official endorsement, he would have neutralized his opposition during the 1944 election.

This episode with Willkie took place from June to August, shortly before the most active part of the campaign against Dewey began. At this point Roosevelt looked old and tired, while Dewey was young and energetic; in fact, "the campaign showed signs of being dull, and perhaps of ending in a Republican victory."[5] Roosevelt probably thought at this time that he needed all the aid he could possibly obtain. As one means of increasing his support, FDR appealed to Willkie, not, of course, on the basis of Republicanism or Democratism, but on the basis of liberalism.

Rosenman explained that when he met with Willkie to discuss the formation of a third party, Willkie said that he wanted to talk about the plan in greater detail with the president, "but he was convinced that the meeting should not take place until after election day. He did not want to appear that he was trading or being traded with; and a meeting between the two before election—

which could not possibly be kept secret—would give rise to many conjectures."[6] Rosenman relayed this information to Roosevelt; yet the president wrote to Willkie, his former Republican opponent, that he wanted to meet with him *before* the election.[7]

This letter to Willkie was so secret that Rosenman says he did not learn of it until a month later, and that probably no one except FDR and Grace Tully, who typed it, knew about it at the time it was sent. Then Rosenman significantly adds: "On this occasion, however, he could not keep the secret himself. He must have talked to someone about the letter, for the fact that it had been sent began to 'leak.' The Willkie adherents charged that the President had deliberately let it leak; the President's supporters insinuated that Willkie had let it leak. Although Roosevelt loved secrecy, he was often the one guilty of letting facts get out about which he had sworn others to silence."[8]

If Roosevelt really wanted to start a new party after the 1944 election, we should ask, first, why would he insist on meeting with Willkie before the election? Rosenman argued that possibly the prospect of a new party was "too thrilling" to allow FDR to wait, but he also admitted that "maybe his motive was—as his hostile critics urged at the time—to give the impression that Willkie was going to support him in the coming 1944 election."[9] Second, we should ask why Roosevelt allowed news of his proposed meeting with Willkie to leak. Rosenman guessed that the news leak was due probably to "some casual remark" of the president's.[10] I think the charge of the Willkie supporters, that the news leak was deliberate, was possibly closer to the truth.

Roosevelt and Willkie never met before the election to discuss the proposal for a new party. However, the attempt to win this prominent Republican's support still partially succeeded. After his sudden death, reports Denis W. Brogan, "some leading Willkieites did come out for the President; others went further and declared that the dead leader had been planning to endorse Roosevelt."[11]

When the actual campaign began in September, the president proved to be a strenuous and inexhaustible man, not a tired old one. "This *tour de force*," says Frank Freidel, "seemingly proving Roosevelt's capacity to serve four more years, his international leadership, and his promise to return to the New Deal after the war, were a winning combination."[12] When the results were in, the Roosevelt magic had marshalled 432 electoral votes to Dewey's 99. Although the belief by some that Willkie would have endorsed Roosevelt did not become a crucial factor in the election, the supposed endorsement did no doubt add to Roosevelt's margin of victory; and, in the dark campaign days of July and August, the winning of Willkie's support probably seemed important to FDR. It was certainly important to Dewey, who had felt, as the campaign reached its climax, that "a word from Willkie . . . [was] a boon greatly to be desired."[13]

In a very subtle manner, Roosevelt had used the liberal label to attract, or appear to attract, a prominent Republican who would have been repelled by the term "Democratic." "Liberal," by Roosevelt's definition, stood for a loose system of ideas that allowed some Republicans to justify their vote for a Democrat.

6

The Epilogue to the Great Debate

The Liberal Symbol after the Roosevelt Era

As we have seen, although the political label "liberal" was introduced into England in 1830, the word was not an important political symbol in the United States until the time of the New Deal. The term had been used occasionally in America before the New Deal, but it had not become a significant or viable word for the great majority of the people.

The *New Republic* did, however, begin using the word "liberal" in 1916. In the later 1920s some left-wing, reformist elements on the periphery of society also began to call themselves liberal. Because of these influences, because "liberal" is an inherently good word that captures the drift of modern history, and also because of identification with the British Liberal party, FDR unconsciously chose to call himself liberal. This political tag not only fulfilled important functions, but it was also the basis for a great debate with the conservative elements of society, represented by Herbert Hoover.

Although Hoover always claimed that he was the true liberal, by the 1936 election the articulate public generally probably agreed—even though the debate over the term continued until about 1940—that the new label "liberal" should be applied to Roosevelt's new policies, which transcended much American tradition. Since "liberal" had stood for Roosevelt's experimentation, which led to his entire philosophy of positive governmental action, that political tag is still a frequently used symbol today. However, since "New Deal" has been associated, not with

Roosevelt's policies, but with Roosevelt's administration, that term is no longer important.

Beginning in 1936, some conservatives admitted that Roosevelt had captured "liberal," and they accepted the label of "conservative." The Court-packing plan of 1937 seemingly interrupted this trend, but it actually helped its continuance, because the Court proposal made New Deal liberalism even more suspect in the eyes of conservatives. After the failure of the Court-packing plan the trend resumed, and some conservatives began to accept more readily the name of "conservative."

By 1940, the actual debate was over for the great majority of people. The articulate public in general agreed that Roosevelt's policies should be called "liberal" and that Hoover's should properly be labeled "conservative." But as the term "liberal" became more and more closely associated with the policies of the New Deal and the Fair Deal, the political tag became less seductive; it lost some of its inherent power. As conservatives accepted the fact that their opponents were named liberal, they reduced their effort to win the word "liberal" and instead focused their attacks on the substantive policies of the liberals.

Early in 1949, for example, the *New York Herald Tribune* asked its readers to send in their own definitions of "liberal." Replies ranged from "one who wants someone else to support him, to think for him . . . to protect him from those who would impose on him responsibilities," to "a liberal is a man who is constantly and simultaneously being kicked in the teeth by the Commies and in the pants by the National Association of Manufacturers." Although the great majority still considered the term to be one of honor, a few thought the label to be degrading.[1] "Liberal," then, was on the whole still an advantageous word to own, but the strong conservatives were able to reject what they felt was a derogatory designation.

Later, when President Eisenhower assumed office, he continued this trend, for he "told us not to be afraid of the word 'conservative.'" However, he still tried to mitigate the impact of the symbol and conducted what James W. Prothro called an "incomplete search, despite the assistance of some of the country's most efficient advertising men, for an appropriate slogan to describe his public philosophy—with 'progressive moderation' being replaced by the equally equivocal 'dynamic conservatism' [reflecting] . . . at least an uneasiness about the appeal of Hoover-style Republicanism."[2]

Though conservatives during the Eisenhower years rejected the term "liberal," they realized that the "conservative" tag then lacked the inherent drawing power of "liberal." Even Barry Goldwater, a man proud of his conservatism, revealed his frustration that conservatives were not called liberal. As late as 1963, when addressing an enthusiastic audience of Young Republicans, he charged that "the young people of America are sick and tired of the phoniness that has been going on under the false guise of liberalism for the last thirty years." Later in this speech he added, "Modern liberalism is only a form of rigor mortis. The old, respectable, sometimes noble liberalism of fifty years ago is gone for good."[3]

Indeed, Hoover's definition of liberalism seemed gone for good as far as the general public was concerned. The best the conservatives could do was to try to popularize their tag. Eisenhower and especially Goldwater in effect tried to do this. The business community represented by *Fortune* magazine also understood the need to breathe a better meaning into their "conservative" label. As one author realized:

> One of the most important facts of life is that a rose by another name does *not* smell as sweet. It is time to get our labels clear.
>
> To sum up: If "conservative" means a love of adventure, a deep concern for opportunity, a recognition of the need for tolerance and change, then I say, "If this be conservatism—make the most of it." But if "conservative" means a love of routine, a love of status and security, a denial of opportunity, reverence for the status quo, then like the other "Virginian" I say, "When you call me that, *smile!*"[4]

A clear sign that the general debate over the proper definition of liberalism was muted, if not virtually dead, is that attacks on the use of the word have been virtually ignored by the popular press. For example, Robert A. Taft, in 1946, argued that he was really liberal and that "self-styled liberals" advocated the continuation of the Office of Price Administration, Truman's proposal for compulsory federal health insurance, and peacetime conscription, which were "three essentially totalitarian measures."[5] Although a business newspaper proudly printed the entire speech in which he presented his contentions, the general public was not even stirred enough to ask, "Who is really liberal?" Several years later one conservative writer charged that the word "liberal" no longer meant "a citizen who had a fixed and shining ideal, a man of honor, a man of logic and clear thought," but now meant "a somewhat confused and craven creature who spends most of his waking hours trying to 'see all sides of the question' and ends up as a confused and ineffectual pulp, whose greatest terror is of being called 'conservative.'"[6] The general press also ignored that attack; it was no longer newsworthy.

The Rise of the Conservative Label

Today it seems that it is the liberals who are in disarray, with the conservative political tag in the ascendancy, along with current buzzwords such as supply-side economics, flat-rate income tax, balanced budgets, and static revenues. How did it come to be that a political label loaded with such favorable connotations could suffer so dramatic a reversal in popularity? The fashionable symbol today is not "liberal" but "conservative" or "libertarian." The pendulum has certainly shifted, but why? Roosevelt's capture of the liberal label has certainly been complete, but the victory has proven hollow. Why?

First, the symbol has become overused. As the breadth of its coverage has increased, the depth of its power has lessened. Like a currency that has become grossly inflated and diluted, the liberal tag has lost much of its power as it has been used to represent support of such widely divergent issues as minimum wage laws, government funding of abortions, and the end of the prohibition of marijuana.

Second, Roosevelt's substantive liberal philosophy has essentially won. As the executive director of the Americans for Democratic Action acknowledged a few years ago, "a substantial number of people are really quite affluent now—economic issues don't impinge the way they did 20 or 30 years ago." The concerns today are not breadlines, sweatshops, unpaid vacations, and excess profits. The focus is rather on bureaucracy, bloated government, overregulation, and high taxes. Liberalism has been one of the victims of its own success as the social agenda has shifted.[7]

In an article ominously entitled, "Update Liberalism, Or It's a 60's Relic," the junior Democratic senator from Massachusetts, Paul E. Tsongas, essentially agreed with the ADA evaluation:

> Liberals must take a fresh look at how to mobilize this new generation. The average young American takes for granted the social equities for which others fought. Young citizens have never known the abuses and injustices that molded older generations of liberals. They have never felt the anger and outrage that fueled the liberal cause. They have not grown up reading about hungry poor people; they have read about abuses in the food-stamp program. They have not grown up confident in an ever-expanding economy; they have seen sagging productivity, record interest rates, and foreign dominance in trade ranging from crude oil to efficient cars. They may remember military adventurism in Vietnam, but they can read every day about Soviet military adventurism in Afghanistan.[8]

Senator Tsongas has been widely regarded as a liberal, with a liberal voting record representing a liberal state. Yet he shifted labels. At first he called his political beliefs the "new liberalism." Then he called it "humane realism." Then he turned to "compassionate realism."[9] The important point is that the various proposed new labels drop the old label of liberal.

Strong evidence demonstrating that FDR's brand of liberal politics has basically won is found in a wide variety of polls that show that many people who now label themselves as conservative nonetheless favor government funding of abortions, federal efforts to provide Medicare and unemployment compensation, and federal regulation of employment safety.[10] In 1964—the year of Barry Goldwater's massive defeat at the polls—only 30 percent of the people called themselves "moderately conservative" or "very conservative." By 1978, 42 percent of the respondents put themselves in this category.[11] However, while the number of self-described conservatives has risen, by 1978 the substantive economic differences between those described as liberal versus those described as conservative seemed to have diminished. For example, about 90 percent of the self-styled liberals believed that the government ought to help people get medical care at low cost. But slightly more than 80 percent of the self-styled conservatives agreed as well. About 80 percent of the self-styled liberals and 70 percent of the self-styled conservatives agreed that the government ought to see to it that everybody who wants a job can get one.[12] Only on a very few social issues was there sharp disagreement: about 65 percent of the self-styled conservatives but only about 45 percent of the self-styled liberals believed that the government should restrict the sale of marijuana if the substance is dangerous.[13] Yesterday's battles become today's truisms, as traditional liberalism becomes a victim of its own success.

Third, the national focus has shifted from the liberal label simply because it is natural for the focus to shift. The tide in the affairs of humankind is not always high tide. As the historian Robert McElvaine has noted, the country's political history has been one of periods of liberal reform punctuated by what he calls "conservative breathing spaces."[14] As the national focus moved from Lyndon Johnson's War on Poverty to the fight for a balanced budget, there was a need to change the arsenal of labels to wage these very different political wars.

Human life seems to revolve around cycles—the twenty-four-hour day, the seven-day week, the four seasons, the twelve-month year. Economics also has its cycles of boom and bust, inflation and recession.

And politics too has its cycles. After the excitement of the Progressives like Teddy Roosevelt and Woodrow Wilson came the normalcy of Coolidge and Harding. The New Deal of Roosevelt and Truman preceded the calmer Eisenhower years. After the era we now nostalgically remember as the 1950s came the elegance of John Fitzgerald Kennedy and the excitement of Camelot. Then came the Great Society and President Lyndon Johnson's crushing victory over the Republican standard-bearer, the proud conservative, Barry Goldwater. Goldwater unashamedly embraced the conservative label, and Johnson tarred him with it. It seemed as though liberalism had reached new pinnacles. And so it had, but the next direction from a summit is down. The horrors of the Vietnam War soon eclipsed the Great Society and gave liberalism a bad name. Well-known liberals such as Hubert Humphrey and Lyndon Johnson embraced the war. Even when other liberals such as Robert Kennedy and Eugene McCarthy attacked it, those attacks also added some bad connotations to the liberal symbol, for some contemporaries labeled these attacks as unpatriotic. And the efforts of the liberals to prevent escalation of the war were seen by some as efforts to have the United States fight with one hand tied behind its back.

The Vietnam War continued under Richard Nixon. Nixon's vice-president, Spiro T. Agnew, knew the importance of words. Agnew spent a great deal of time trying to link "liberal" with "radical." Nixon's second term not only brought more war and Agnew's criminal indictment and resignation; it also brought Watergate—that American drama that the late Senator Sam Ervin thought was more tragic than even the Civil War, for the Civil War saw acts of heroism, honor, and bravery on both sides, and Watergate had no such redeeming features.

After Nixon's near-impeachment and actual resignation, our country's first appointed president and vice-president took office. President Gerald Ford inherited unprecedented inflation, recession, and energy shortages. Ford's successor, Jimmy Carter, added to this triumvirate of problems the Iranian hostage crisis. It was the winter of his discontent.

And then came the Great Communicator. Like Barry Goldwater, Ronald Reagan was not afraid to call himself conservative. But unlike Goldwater, he spent no great effort seeking to dismantle the Tennessee Valley Authority. Rather than refight the lost battles of the New Deal, Reagan unabashedly quoted FDR, while fighting for his new conservative agenda, which included Kennedy-style tax cuts.

This "inherent cyclical rhythm in our public affairs," as Arthur M. Schlesinger, Jr., has said,[15] is reflected in our current fashion in labels. The fact that "conservative" is now a more fashionable

word is strong evidence that President Reagan's election and decisive reelection victory were not merely personal victories but
portended possible fundamental changes in the political mood.
Republicans such as Representative Jack Kemp and Democrats
such as Senator Paul Tsongas have talked of such a realignment,
and recent polls lend some support to that view.[16]

This cyclical rhythm is also reflected in the change in direction
of the *New Republic*. As the *New Republic* turned seventy in 1984,
President Reagan sent it words of praise, while Jeane Kirkpatrick
and Henry Kissinger joined in. Many well-known liberals, such
as Frank Mankiewicz, the former campaign manager for George
McGovern, acknowledge that the *New Republic* has been "getting conservative for some time, but now it's coming out of the
closet." And Republican Representative Jack Kemp agrees:
"There is no question that the *New Republic* is moving in the,
shall we say, right direction." Liberal columnist Nicholas Von
Hoffman bemoans the fact that "this society has no left—except
in baseball. It's very hard to go against fashion—even at the *New
Republic*."[17]

The importance of the liberal label has lessened as the word
has been overused, as the traditional liberal policies have become truisms and liberalism has become a victim of its own success, and as the natural cyclical rhythm has progressed. There
has thus been a dramatic decline in the power of the liberal symbol. Yet it is a tribute to the potency of the liberal label that the
New Right, the proselytizing conservatives, often call themselves "libertarians." Both the Left and the Right find their roots
in the same symbol. And even today the liberal label occasionally
sparks a dispute for its ownership.

Lessons from History

Liberals had won their label, although time has
diminished the value of the victory. And conservatives, who ini-
tially merely accepted their appellation, now relish it. But before
this period, the battle over these symbols reflected and helped
mold the substantive policy disputes.

Roosevelt's adviser, Thurmond Arnold, recognized the significance of the battle over the ownership of symbols when he noted:

> The question which confronts the student of government is what kind of social philosophy is required to make men free to experiment—to give them an understanding of the world, undistorted by the thick prismatic lenses of principles and ideals, and at the same time undamaged by the disillusionment which comes from the abandonment of ideals. How may we make the truths of which men are dimly aware only in humorous or satirical moods into constructive forces to avoid senseless panic when old principles meet new conditions? How may we affect the attitude of that great mass of substantial, intelligent, idealistic, and kindly people whose opinions and actions count most in times of stability, so that they will cease to see impending moral chaos in practical and humanitarian action?[18]

Arnold's statement outlined Roosevelt's problem. The great majority of people had repudiated Hoover's policies in 1932; yet, FDR still needed a new symbol to make his "bold, persistent experimentation" acceptable. "Liberal" was the most appropriate symbol for Roosevelt's purposes and the one he unconsciously chose.

Reliance on the new label was an important means of warding off strong charges from the Right that the New Deal was socialistic and that therefore Roosevelt was planning to regiment society and nationalize industry. If FDR had accepted the designation of Socialist instead of capturing "liberal," he would have lost many followers. The new and favorable term was also an important means of counteracting conservative symbols and of increasing Roosevelt's basis of electoral support. The symbol acted as a counterpressure to the symbol of Republican party identification.

Yet, while this symbol performed these important functions, it could not in itself be a substitute for good policies. "Liberal" proved to be a good label to place on the New Deal package, but Roosevelt still had to prove that the package was worth buying. The use of the label, however, did allow the public in general to examine the New Deal's policies on its merits, "unencumbered by constant thoughts of impending moral chaos."[19] Roosevelt's use of his political tag answered the questions that Arnold had asked.

Several of Roosevelt's contemporary critics asserted that FDR's capture of "liberal" was an important factor in his election victories. To be sure, "liberal" was an important and favorable political term, but it had its limits. The failure of the purge of 1938 was one incident that clearly illustrated the limits of the power of the word, for Roosevelt's label proved to be an insufficient basis on which to realign American political parties. In modern times, as the national mood has become more conservative, we can more easily appreciate that the liberal label has lost much of its seductive power.

An appreciation of the origins and development of the political symbol "liberal" should also make us more cautious in applying modern labels, with all the verbal baggage that they carry, as a means of trying to understand and interpret the past. Raymond Poincaré, the president of France from 1913 to 1920, had warned that "we have to make use of language, which is made up necessarily of preconceived ideas. Such ideas unconsciously held are the most dangerous of all." And Bentham added, "error is never so difficult to be destroyed as when it has its roots in language."[20] Words not only reflect but also determine people's thinking. Hence, we must be aware of the importance of words in order to consider their power to determine our thoughts. For example, scholars have occasionally labeled a past historical figure as liberal, and have erroneously assumed that class-conscious electoral politics or similar aspects of the New Deal would naturally be exported along with the political label. As Thomas P. Neill has prudently warned: "Now an abstraction like ["liberal"] creates difficulties for the historian. He is concerned with ideas as they are held by concrete persons at given times and places in history. He must be careful not to read his own or his age's understanding of a word back into the minds of men using the same word three or four generations ago. . . . If an historian were to do this he would fall into the trap of analyzing the wine in the bottles. He must also be careful not to transfer the contents of the term from one country to another."[21]

I would add that, while scholars must be careful not to read a modern definition into the past's use of the word, they must also exercise great care when reading a modern word and all that it implies into a past that did not even use the word. Symbols are not only the hidden persuaders; they can be the hidden confusers.

Our study of the rise and decline of the liberal label should demonstrate, in a very concrete way, the importance of symbols in law and government. There are limits to the power of symbols. But there is also a magic in words: not the magic of "abracadabra," but magic nonetheless. Words have the ability to confuse and to clarify, to help legitimate policies, to generate loyalty, to give the appearance of action, to mold people's perceptions of the world, to affect the way they approach a problem, and to reflect their innermost thoughts.

When people argue about "mere words," they are talking about fundamentals, about infrastructure, not superstructure. As the prophet John said, "In the Beginning was the Word."

Afterword: The Format of Legal and Political Discourse

M. H. Hoeflich

Normativity and Instrumentalism

Several stimuli have sparked this essay and the case study that precedes it. First, they have developed from a close reading of H. L. A. Hart's now classic (and still controversial) *The Concept of Law*[1] and two brief commentaries on it, A. M. Honoré's "Real Laws" and R. S. Summers's "Naive Instrumentalism and the Law," both published in Professor Hart's festschrift, *Law, Morality, and Society.*[2] After twenty-one years Professor Hart's insights, expounded in *The Concept of Law*, remain fresh. It is the great genius of this book that his insights into the "social sources of law" are often not fully delineated and are even ambiguous, for it is this lack of final resolution that makes the book a starting point for discussion rather than the last word on the subject. The second impetus for this essay is a growing conviction that the economic approach to law, insofar as it points out the necessity of considering the economic logic of legal rules and doctrines, at least convinces us to focus upon issues such as the social cost of alternative legal mechanisms, the allocation of scarce societal resources, and indeed the efficiency of our whole legal structure, which for too long have been ignored by legal scholars. Third, it has grown from a reading of much of the recent output of those scholars who are members of the Critical Legal Studies Group and the attention they have drawn to the necessity of using semiological, structuralist, and other linguistic tools to understand law in its social context.[3] It is thus the purpose of this essay to attempt, in a small way, a cross-fertilization of analytic jurisprudence and legal economics on the one hand, and analytic linguistics on the other, focused on the forms of legal discourse and how these forms function within society.

Central to Professor Hart's idea of law is a rejection of the Benthamite and Austinian notion that law, stripped to its bare essentials, is a series of commands, expressions of the will of a sovereign, backed by the threat of sanctions.[4] Professor Hart, borrowing from the insights of modern sociologists, has rejected this simplistic definition of law and developed instead the notion of law as a system of normative rules.[5] This notion of normativity is extraordinarily fruitful. Normativity is, above all, a social concept. A rule is normative if it is one that a significant portion of a populace believes to state and create an obligation to behave in a certain way.[6] By "obligation" is meant that a significant part of society accepts that the rule *ought* to be obeyed and that disobedience to the rule is ipso facto blameworthy and therefore worthy of censure.[7] A normative rule will be the focus of "serious social pressure" in favor of compliance.[8] Normativity does *not* guarantee that a rule will be obeyed. Rather, it means that members of the group for which the rule is normative possess what Professor Hart has called "an internal point of view" and can make comments upon the "internal aspect" of normative rules.[9] Thus, although normativity does not guarantee compliance, it does signify that an individual violating a normative rule would recognize that, in the eyes of society, his act was wrong and blameworthy and that were he censured or sanctioned, he would deserve it. Normative rules, therefore, involve an internalization of a specific attitude inclining individuals to compliance and acceptance of situations where compliance, at least in the short run, may run counter to specific personal goals. Acceptance of normative rules may, in fact, require instances of renunciation or sacrifice or, in crude economic terms, nonutility maximization over the short term.[10]

The focus of this notion of normativity is society. Normativity is a social fact, discoverable by an external observer. In this view of law, normative rules may be seen as one interface between society and society's ideas of how it wishes to shape itself. The discovery of a society's normative rules will tell us much about that society, how it functions, and how it sees itself.

It is clear that normativity may take a number of forms in terms of obligation-creating statements. For instance, a rule may be morally normative or it may be legally normative. Professor Hart would make a distinction between these two types of normative rules based not on some difference in their "internal aspects," for there is none, but rather in their context.[11] He would suggest that a rule is legally normative because of its "systematic" nature, its place within the union of different types of rules that he labels primary and secondary.[12] It is this systematic aspect of some rules that leads Professor Hart to characterize them as legal. This distinction and its focus on the systematic nature of so-called legal rules has not been without its critics, but one might suggest that this distinction is neither always clear, even if it is fundamentally sound, nor necessarily significant. Many rules may be normative in more than one way. Thus a rule might be both morally normative and legally normative. Think, for instance, of the general social prohibition of father-daughter incest in the United States. This prohibition is certainly legally normative, for it is a fundamental rule of criminal and family law and an integral part of our legal system. But it is also certainly morally normative, for even were there no legal prohibition of father-daughter incest, there would remain "serious social pressure" against such relations, springing from our common Judaeo-Christian morality. Indeed, one might argue that the particular strength of certain rules comes from their multiple normativity. Thus, rules prohibiting father-daughter incest are perhaps stronger in their social context than rules prohibiting insider stock trading, although both rules are legally normative. By "strength" I mean only the degree to which a sense of obligation attaches itself to a particular rule and the degree to which deviation from a particular rule will be held blameworthy. The stock trader may be sanctioned while the promoter of incest may be shunned. So, too, perhaps, if public morality ever develops strongly in a direction opposed to pollution of the environment, environmental laws may gain in strength. The question would seem to be one of degree.

Having now arrived at this simple concept of legal normativity, we may now add the next element: instrumentalism, indeed what Professor Summers has called "naive instrumentalism."[13] Instrumentalism is the doctrine that laws should be
oriented so as to achieve specific social goals. It is sociological
teleology. "Naive instrumentalism," as Professor Summers de-
fines it, may be expressed as follows: "We have laws to serve social goals—communal functions. When officials set a goal and
pass a law, the idea [is] to achieve, more or less directly, a specific
end result (goal) by changing the behavior of people. The law
tells people what to do (provides guidance) and says what will
happen if they fail (usually some kind of punishment). Thus,
every effective law brings about social change. And it is officials
who make the law effective by enforcing it."[14]

This definition of naive instrumentalism clearly will not do
if the purpose of the definition is to provide a complete description of law or legal system. However, the notion of naive instrumentalism can still be quite useful, for it does describe a particular approach to law and legal rules.

American legal historians have demonstrated during the past
decade that the attitudes of many American lawyers, legislators,
and judges toward the law were highly instrumental.[15] In broad
perspective, law was seen as a tool, a means by which commerce, industry, and other commonly agreed-upon political and
social goals could be facilitated.[16] To a large degree, it would appear that these individuals' attitudes toward law in the nineteenth century could easily be characterized as naive instrumentalism. Again, in the twentieth century, those individuals who
used law in implementing the New Deal could easily be characterized as naive instrumentalists. For them law was a primary
means of effecting "social engineering." In short, one might suggest that a fundamental difference between the attitude of naive
instrumentalism and the more sophisticated and complex per-
spectives of modern legal philosophers is that the naive instrumentalist determines that law, in certain circumstances, may be
used as an instrument of social control, as a means of effecting
essentially political or economic ends. Obviously, this view of
law is rather far removed from notions of law either as a system

of rules distinct from politics or morality or as a system of rules designed to facilitate populist, libertarian, and individualistic ends. Similarly, it seems at odds with any notion of law as a set of normative rules. On the contrary, it is a view that opponents might characterize as elitist. Nevertheless, it is a view that has been held by many individuals both earlier in our history and today. These people, the "educated laity," as Professor Summers calls them, see law as a social and political tool.[17] This view, one may argue, is one that is especially defensible today, on the grounds that our nation is entering a period of social heterogeneity and breakdown of traditional order, thereby requiring a reinforcement of "law and order." Indeed, one issue often taken with the Hartian, sociological perspective is that it lacks direction or teleology. It is essentially neutral, removed from politics and political goals.

The great difficulty with the naive instrumentalist view, however, is that it perceives law to be an instrument of hierarchy, imposed upon a populace by its officials. Thus, naive instrumentalism hearkens back to the Benthamite and Austinian view of law as commands issued by a sovereign and backed by sanctions.[18] One might suggest that this connection between the naive instrumentalist view and the Benthamite "sanction theory" of law is not logically necessary or desirable, for the latter presupposes a legal system wherein the costs of enforcement in a large, heterogeneous society may well be enormous and require the establishment of a state enforcement system that itself requires a substantial portion of a society's resources.[19] In addition to these potentially enormous economic costs, there are other costs, such as the potential loss of individual privacy and the breakdown in trust in the disinterestedness of governmental and legal officials. The imposition of rules by authorities upon a populace that has not internalized a sense of obligation to obey such rules is economically and socially inefficient; if fear of sanctions is the sole or even primary motivation for obedience, then this fear must be maintained. Maintenance of such a fear among a large population is simply too costly in its use of resources. Put differently, a system of imposed rules of behavior lacking the backing of a serious social pressure toward obedience simply

cannot be effectively maintained at an acceptable cost. Furthermore, such a system has echoes of totalitarianism and is likely to
be politically unacceptable in so blatant a form.

To return to the nineteenth-century instrumentalist development of law for a moment, it is necessary to understand the reason why certain social groups were able to shape the law in
directions that facilitated those groups' nonlegal ends. One can
posit at least two possible scenarios. The first is that law was, in
fact, an instrument of repression used by the more powerful elements in society against other social groups that were incapable
of defending themselves or shaping the law to their different
ends. Certainly laws oriented to the detriment of minorities,
such as blacks, would fit within this category.[20] Alternatively, one
may see the instrumental nature of the substantive legal changes
as part of a broader package, including an ideology and frame-
work that made it acceptable to most people, regardless of their
particular self-interest. In other words, one might suggest that
the nineteenth-century instrumentalists were successful politically because they were able to clothe their legal programs in
normativity, i.e., convince a substantial portion of the American
populace that their legal program was what it wanted.

It is at this point that we may return to the Hartian concept of
normativity for assistance. Professor Hart notes in his preface to
The Concept of Law that his study is one of legal sociology. The
description of normative rule statements that he develops is not
inductive; rather, it is empirical and based upon a close analysis
of common, everyday language. Ultimately, norms are not theo-
retical constructs. They are social facts. A normative rule statement is a verbal description of a social fact relating to accepted
modes of social behavior and social obligations. Thus, the notion of a normative rule statement is quite different from the
notion of a rule as defined by a sanction theorist. Of course, Professor Hart does not expect that all members of a society will
share the "internal point of view" necessary to the existence of a
valid norm in relation to all rule statements. Indeed, he avoids
this absurd proposition by building two qualities into his description of law: a systematic quality and a hierarchic quality.[21]
He calls the systematic quality the "union of primary and secondary rules."[22] By this he means that a legal system will not

consist solely of normative rule statements giving rise to obligations but will also contain other types of rules—what he calls rules of recognition, change, and adjudication.[23] It is these rules—labeled "secondary" by Professor Hart—that give a systematic quality to law; they establish legal processes and procedures for legal creation and enforcement. The hierarchic quality built into Professor Hart's theory of law derives from his belief that a group smaller than the whole of society may, in fact, recognize the normative aspect of rule statements, while the remainder of society will obey such rules for fear of the imposition of sanctions or similar forms of compulsion. Professor Hart postulates an extreme case where only the "official" class in society shares an internal point of view towards rules, while all other members obey for other reasons. In his view, such a system is still a legal/normative system so long as the officials, those who must create and enforce legal rules, regard such rules as norms. In this extreme case, the normative rule statements are social facts within this official class alone.

It becomes clear that in the extreme case the view of law in society espoused by Professor Hart begins to resemble the view of law that we have attributed to a "sanction theorist." In Professor Hart's extreme case, the official class faces the same dilemma in regard to enforcement costs and political resistance in a large and heterogeneous society as would the sovereign in the view of the sanction theorist. Professor Hart's theory of normativity, however, if not pushed to the extreme case, may provide the foundation for deriving a partial solution to the problem of enforcement costs and to creating a viable theory of legal instrumentalism. To the extent that a legal rule is normative—that is, it is backed by serious social pressure and therefore exists as a social fact within a large segment of society—enforcement costs borne by government (or the dominant social group promoting the rule) ought to lessen substantially. They should do so because legal officials (the "sovereigns") cease to be the sole enforcers of the rules. If a normative rule exists within society, then by definition, strong social pressure will be exerted by all members of the society sharing the internal point of view as to that rule in favor of obedience. Such pressure does *not* ensure that rules will always be obeyed, but it does mean that most people will obey such rules most of the time, i.e., they will be law-abiding. Furthermore, there will be a large segment of society ready to discover deviations from the rule. To the extent that legal rules can be normative, one ought to see the phenomenon of a self-enforcement process, which will be less costly from an economic perspective though perhaps not less intrusive from a privacy perspective.[24] The legal system, as a result, will be able to operate more cost-effectively.

As already noted, however, normativity is a social fact, one that arises within society. It cannot simply be imposed by governmental fiat. A sovereign or its agents cannot simply declare that henceforth a particular rule will be normative and seriously expect that it will be so. Nevertheless, sovereigns and officials—those having the power and authority to make and enforce law—must recognize the cost efficiency of normative rules and attempt to foster normativity and not depend solely on the fear of sanctions and deterrence. This, we may suggest, can be accomplished in part by shaping the perception of particular substantive legal rules by members of a society through careful attention to the forms of legal discourse and by adopting an ideological and explanatory context for the rules designed to make them more acceptable, thereby facilitating the process of internalization. To return to the nineteenth century, one may suggest that the precise reason why legal instrumentalism in favor of commercial interests was so successful was because substantive law changes were presented within a particular style of judicial reasoning, which has come to be known since Llewellyn as "legal formalism."[25] Substantive tort law changes were not baldly pronounced as being for the benefit of the railroads, for instance. Rather, the rules were "derived" from "established doctrine."[26] By this means, it became necessary for the populace to internalize a belief in the inexorable logic and progress of the law in order to give normative value to these substantive changes.

The Modern Instrumentalist

The legal instrumentalist in the latter part of the twentieth century faces a number of problems that our nineteenth-century predecessors avoided. First, society is infinitely more complex, and the legislative and judicial institutions of society have correspondingly grown more complex, larger, and more heterogeneous. And, of course, our society and the groups holding political and legal power in it have grown more numerous and far more heterogeneous. Nevertheless, instrumentalism in the sense described above is not impossible in the modern context. What has changed radically from the nineteenth- to the twentieth-century contexts, however, is the relative merit of attempting to establish hierarchically imposed sets of legal rules over an unwilling or disinterested populace, as opposed to attempting to create an environment conducive to internalization of desired legal changes. If broad internalization of desired rules can be achieved in a heterogeneous and large society, it would seem quite reasonable that the social cost of implementing these legal changes would be far lower than any attempt simply to impose them on an unwilling or disinterested group. For one, in the latter case compliance costs will be higher the larger and more complex a society becomes. Second, as a society becomes more complex, strict enforcement of noninternalized rules becomes far more difficult, and the level of intrusiveness necessary to achieve satisfactory compliance may be deemed by the populace to be too high to be acceptable. Such a phenomenon currently plagues tax policymakers confronting compliance issues in the industrialized West.[27] To maximize economic efficiency as well as minimize governmental intrusiveness in private affairs, it would seem desirable to employ any method by which internalization of legal rules in a large and complex society could be facilitated.

This, of course, raises the question of whether any such effective method exists. Certainly, heterogeneity is a factor counter to the success of any means used to facilitate popular internalization of legal rules and the creation of "Hartian" norms. One aspect of Professor Hart's *Concept of Law* that has received too little attention is the fact that the social model he develops is based, in large part, on mid-twentieth-century England, one of the least heterogeneous populations in the West. Internalization of legal rules and the development of norms with the concomitant creation of serious social pressure against deviation from those norms presupposes a society sharing at least certain fundamental ideas and premises. In the United States, for much of this century, we have witnessed a growing cultural and social heterogeneity as well as the disappearance of many fundamental, shared concepts. The agony of the Vietnam experience and the disillusionment of Watergate and its aftermath have combined to shatter even the most basic concepts to which most Americans might once have subscribed. Thus, there is some question whether it is possible at all, in our current society, to find a means of facilitating widespread internalization and norm-creation. Professor Rotunda's study of the development and use of the idea of liberalism in American political and legal circles in the late nineteenth century and first half of the twentieth century is an attempt to explore this question.

Instrumentalism and the Study of Political/Legal Terms

The text that precedes this essay contains a case study of how one particular political/legal term became integral to the American political tradition over time. Its importance lies in two areas. First, it is an excellent attempt to examine how, over the course of several centuries, the notions of "liberal" and "liberalism" took on significant connotative values. Words, generally, may have both denotative and connotative values. Their denotative values are their core meanings. Their connotative values are more complex. These are the images, the interconnections with other concepts, the subtleties and shades of meaning a particular word may give rise to in the minds of a reader or listener. Denotative values change slowly, if at all. Connotative values, however, must be understood within particular socio-historical contexts—must be seen, indeed, as outgrowths of those contexts. The connotative values of a particular term are, in this sense, normative and are observable social facts. Thus, on one level, that of historical inquiry, the preceding case study of the changes in the social meanings and impact of the terms "liberal" and "liberalism" is of great significance. It allows us to see how a basic political/legal term has had varied connotations during different periods and in different societies, precisely in response to those societies' normative beliefs.[28]

The second level on which this case study is of great significance relates to the first two parts of this essay. The notions of "liberal" and "liberalism" are not clear-cut in our society. The case study might easily have been subtitled "A Study in Ambiguity." Nevertheless, these terms have connotations that make them fundamentally legitimizing for a significant part of the American populace, just as does the term "conservative" for another part. Thus, to label a particular political or legal action as liberal, regardless of the true substance of the action, will affect how that action is received by different parts of society. To take an illustrative example, let us suppose that the Supreme Court keeps its promise and next year decides a case turning upon the continued validity of the exclusionary rule. Let us also suppose that the Court decides effectively to retain the exclusionary rule in American jurisprudence. That retention will take place in the form of a written opinion, or more likely several opinions. If, in the course of writing such an opinion, the author uses liberal phraseology and portrays the decision as one falling squarely within the liberal American judicial and legal tradition, it seems quite inevitable that the linguistic usages in the opinion will influence the public. Those who hold themselves to be liberals will incline toward acceptance. Those who hold themselves opposed to liberalism will incline toward rejection of the decision. Of course, I do not suggest that labeling the act, in and of itself, will legitimize it, but at the very least it will create a presumption of legitimacy for those who support—indeed have internalized—the label.

Thus, perhaps the core of the Professor Rotunda's study is its examination of the way in which the modern notion of liberalism was first developed and popularized in this country through the writings of Harold Laski and the *New Republic* staff and how Franklin Roosevelt, himself a consummate master of the political arena, used this phrase to aid him in attempting precisely the form of legal shaping so necessary to New Deal social engineering. By examining the degree of success or lack of it, one can gain insight into how much the instrumentalist approach to law can be aided through the use of a carefully chosen linguistic format. Thus, the case study becomes, in fact, a historical testing ground for the notion that the molding of an instrumentalist approach to law, what many might call even an activist approach, can be facilitated through careful shaping and presentation.

Concluding Remarks

One of the most basic questions that even beginning law students always ask is why people obey the pronouncements of legislatures and courts. It is obvious, precisely from the growing breakdown in overall respect for law in its various forms, that this question cannot be answered simply by saying that people obey because they fear sanctions. As noted, to maintain an adequate deterrence system is too costly, both economically and socially. A possible answer is, in the language of nineteenth-century contract lawyers, that people obey laws where they have come to a meeting of the minds with the laws' promulgators, when they have internalized the laws to the point that they have become normative. This study of political/legal language and its use during one of the most legally activist periods in American history helps us to understand how language can facilitate that internalization. Or to be quite blunt, as merchandisers know, public acceptance of a product depends as much on the packaging as on the product itself. For law, the packaging is the language in which it is conceived, written, and explained.

Notes

1. Symbols in Politics and Law

1. Thurmond W. Arnold, *The Symbols of Government* (New Haven: Yale University Press, 1935).

2. Sheldon S. Wolin, *Politics and Vision* (Boston: Little, Brown & Co., 1960), p. 76.

3. See, for example, Kenneth Clark, *The Nude: A Study in Ideal Form* (Garden City, N.Y.: Doubleday & Co., 1956), pp. 227–28.

4. Murray Edelman, *The Symbolic Uses of Politics* (Urbana, Ill.: University of Illinois Press, 1964), p. 19. See, generally, Schauer, *An Essay on Constitutional Language*, 29 U.C.L.A. L. REV. 797 (1982).

5. West Virginia State Board of Education v. Barnette, 319 U.S. 624, 662 (1943) (Frankfurter, J., dissenting). Justice Jackson, in West Virginia State Board of Education v. Barnette, 319 U.S. 624, 632 (1943), in the majority opinion, agreed with Frankfurter's analysis of the importance of symbols. See also Justice Cardozo in Louis K. Liggett Co. v. Lee, 288 U.S. 517, 586 (1933) and, generally, Moore, *The Semantics of Judging*, 54 SO. CALIF. L. REV. 167 (1981).

6. "Kennedy Clashes with CORE Chief," *New York Times*, December 9, 1966, p. 1.

7. T. H. Williams, Richard N. Current, and Frank Freidel, *A History of the United States Since 1865* (New York: Alfred A. Knopf, 1961), p. 197.

8. Ibid., p. 332.

9. Thurmond Arnold, *The Folklore of Capitalism* (New Haven: Yale University Press, 1937), pp. 207–208.

10. Nan Robertson, "Teacher Opposes the Term 'Negro,'" *New York Times*, December 10, 1966, p. 27.

11. Dean Rusk, et al., *The Vietnam Hearings* (New York: Random House, 1966), pp. 137–38. The quotations cited are taken from Mr. Kennan's testimony. See also Stone, *From a Language Perspective*, 90 YALE L.J. 1149 (1981).

12. Edelman, *Symbolic Uses*, p. 122. See also Ellen Peters, *Reality and the Language of Law*, 90 YALE L.J. 1193, 1196 (1981); M. H. Hoeflich, "The

Speculator in the Governmental Theory of the Early Church," *Vigiliae Christianae* 34 (1980): 120, 125, 127; Deutsch and Hoeflich, *Legal Duty and Judicial Style: The Meaning of Precedent*, 25 St. Louis U.L.J. 87 (1981).

13. See, for example, Stanley L. Payne, *The Art of Asking Questions* (Princeton, N.J.: Princeton University Press, 1951).

14. Bertram D. Wolfe, *Three Who Made a Revolution* (New York: Stein and Day, 1964), pp. 243–44.

15. See, for example, William J. Small, *Political Power and the Press* (New York: W. W. Norton & Co., 1972), p. 204.

16. *Time*, November 6, 1972, p. 36.

17. *Army Digest*, April 1968.

18. Cited in Harry Hoijer, "Cultural Implications of Some Navajo Linguistics Categories," in *Language in Culture and Society*, ed. Dell Hymes (New York: Harper and Row, Publishers, 1964), p. 142.

19. Ibid.

20. See Martin Diamond, "The Federalists' View of Federalism," in George C. S. Benson, et al., *Essays in Federalism* (Claremont, Ca.: Institute for Studies in Federalism, 1961), pp. 27–42.

21. Robert G. McCloskey, *American Conservatism in the Age of Enterprise* (Cambridge, Mass.: Harvard University Press, 1951), pp. 168–73.

22. Giovanni Sartori, *Democratic Theory* (New York: Frederick A. Praeger, Inc., 1965), p. 353.

23. Louis Hartz documents the complete lack of appeal of socialism and communism in the United States in his book, *The Liberal Tradition in America* (New York: Harcourt, Brace & World, Inc., 1955).

24. See, for example, O. G. Villard, "What Is a Liberal?" *Nation*, November 27, 1937; M. Thorpe, "Who, Then Is the Liberal? Justice Reynolds and His Decisions," *Saturday Evening Post*, March 12, 1938; E. F. Goldman and M. Paull, "Liberals on Liberalism: Nine Definitions of Liberalism," *New Republic*, July 22, 1946; "What Is a Liberal?" *Time*, February 21, 1949; D. Bendiner, "What Is a Liberal?" *Nation*, March 26, 1949; R. M. Christenson, "What Is a Liberal?" *New Republic*, July 19, 1948. See also Lou Harris, "5% More Call Selves More Liberal," *Washington Post*, November 27, 1972.

25. By 1978, 42 percent of the respondents in a poll called themselves moderately conservative or very conservative. In 1964 only 30 percent of the poll respondents put themselves in that category. Adam Clymer, "More Conservatives Share 'Liberal' View," *New York Times*, January 22, 1978.

26. Adam B. Ulam, *The Unfinished Revolution* (New York: Random House, 1960), p. 90.

27. For example, see Herbert Hoover, *The Challenge to Liberty* (New York: Charles Scribner's Sons, 1934), pp. 3–10; and Robert A. Taft, "What Is a Liberal," *Commercial and Financial Chronicle*, May 16, 1946, pp. 2641, 2668, 2670.

28. Charles Frankel, "A Liberal Is a Liberal Is a—," *New York Times*, February 28, 1960, sect. 6, p. 21.

29. Quoted in Emmet John Hughes, *The Ordeal of Power: A Political Memoir of the Eisenhower Years* (New York: Atheneum, 1963), p. 271.

30. Frankel, "A Liberal."

31. See "Politics and the Name Game," *Time*, November 2, 1970.

32. Alan P. Grimes, "Contemporary American Liberalism," *Annuals of the American Academy of Political and Social Sciences* (November 1962): 33.

33. Erwin L. Linn, "The Influence of Liberalism and Conservatism on Voting Behavior," *Public Opinion Quarterly* 13 (Summer 1949): 299, 300, 307, 309.

34. Grimes, "Contemporary American Liberalism," p. 33.

35. *It's Later Than You Think: The Need for a Militant Democracy* (New York: Viking Press, 1939), p. 3.

36. "The Pragmatic Course of Liberalism," *Western Political Quarterly* 9 (September 1956): 633.

37. See L. T. Hobhouse, *Liberalism* (New York: Henry Holt & Co., 1911).

38. Thomas P. Neill, *The Rise and Decline of Liberalism* (Milwaukee: Bruce Publishing Company, 1953), pp. 279–80.

39. Ibid., p. 283.

40. Guido de Ruggiero, *The History of European Liberalism*, trans. R. G. Collingwood (Boston: Beacon Press, 1959), p. 156.

41. Neill, *Rise and Decline*, pp. 278–79.

42. Herbert Croly, *The Promise of American Life*, ed. Arthur M. Schlesinger, Jr. (1909; reprinted ed., Cambridge, Mass.: Belknap Press of Harvard University Press, 1965), p. v.

43. "Liberalism and the National Idea," in *Left, Right, and Center: Essays on Liberalism and Conservatism in the United States*, ed. Robert A. Goldwin (Chicago: University of Chicago, Public Affairs Conference Center, 1965), p. 143.

44. Franklin D. Roosevelt, *The Public Papers and Addresses of Franklin D. Roosevelt*, ed. Samuel I. Rosenman (New York: Random House [vols. 1–5], Macmillan Co. [vols. 6–9], Harper & Brothers [vols. 10–12], 1938–50).

45. Beer, "Liberalism," p. 144.

46. An article count in the *Readers' Guide to Periodical Literature* shows

that in the ten-year period 1890–99 (when 56 periodicals were indexed) there was only one article indexed under "Liberalism." In the early years of the New Deal, from July 1932 to June 1935, the *Readers' Guide* indexed 114 periodicals and reports. Though the number of indexed materials merely doubled—reflecting in part a more intelligent, more articulate, and more politically aware public—the number of articles listed under "Liberalism" increased by forty times. This figure is made more impressive if we remember that this second time period is less than one-third as long as the first time period.

47. Another index reflecting popular usage and mass vocabulary is the *New York Times Index*. The preface to each volume of the index assures us that the headings reflect the popular concerns of that year. A heading may appear with many articles listed under it one year, and the heading itself may have disappeared the next year. The results of a search through the *New York Times Index*, from 1913 through 1965, demonstrates that it is not until 1922 that the subject heading "Liberalism" is even listed in the index. By far the greatest number of articles concerned with liberalism as a symbol appear in the decade of the 1930s. This article search shows only the number of times articles referring to liberalism were written. What it does not show, and what we will see later, is not only that there were more articles in the New Deal period than any previous time period, but also that many of these articles were much longer and more thorough than previously; full-length magazine articles suddenly appear in the popular literature of the 1930s discussing "liberal" as a political symbol.

48. Personal communication, October 26, 1966.

49. Raymond Moley, with the assistance of Elliot A. Rosen, *The First New Deal* (New York: Harcourt, Brace & World, Inc., 1966), p. 327*n*.

50. Personal communication, December 7, 1966.

51. Personal communication, November 22, 1966.

52. R. G. Tugwell, "The New Deal: The Progressive Tradition," *Western Political Quarterly* 3 (September 1950):420.

53. John T. Flynn, "What Liberalism Means to Me," *American Mercury* 67 (August 1948):175.

54. *New York Times*, February 23, 1936, sect. 7, p. 3.

2. The British Analogy

1. Giovanni Sartori, *Democratic Theory* (New York: Frederick A. Praeger, Inc., 1965), p. 357.

2. See Thomas P. Neill, *The Rise and Decline of Liberalism* (Milwaukee:

Bruce Publishing Company, 1953), p. 7, and Neill, "Liberalism . . . A Term of Many Meanings Whose Sense Must Be Defined When Used," *Social Order* 3–4 (October 1954):341.

3. Neill, "Liberalism," p. 341.

4. Neill, *Rise and Decline*, p. 7.

5. Neill, "Liberalism," p. 341.

6. Sartori, *Democratic Theory*, pp. 357–58.

7. Neill, "Liberalism," p. 341.

8. Neill, *Rise and Decline*, p. 94.

9. Ibid., pp. 94–95.

10. J. M. Robertson, *The Meaning of Liberalism* (London: Kennikat Press, 1925), p. 15.

11. Sir James A. H. Murray, ed., *A New English Dictionary on Historical Principles*, vol. 6 (Oxford: Clarendon Press, 1908), p. 238.

12. Sir William A. Craigie and James R. Hulbert, eds., *A Dictionary of American English: On Historical Principles*, vol. 3 (Chicago: University of Chicago Press, 1942), p. 1417.

13. See Michael Grant, *Roman History from Coins* (Cambridge, Eng.: Cambridge University Press, 1958), for a discussion of Roman use of *Liberalitas* on coins; cf. A. R. Hands, *Charities and Social Aid in Greece and Rome* (Ithaca, N.Y.: Cornell University Press, 1968).

14. Neill, *Rise and Decline*, p. 3.

15. Hamilton Fyfe, *The British Liberal Party* (London: George Allen & Unwin Ltd., 1928), p. 14.

16. Murray, vol. 6, p. 238.

17. The new label "conservative" was also successful because of its appeal to those fearful of the violent changes occurring in France. Robertson, *The Meaning of Liberalism*, p. 14.

18. Sir James A. H. Murray, ed., *A New English Dictionary on Historical Principles*, vol. 2 (Oxford: Clarendon Press, 1893), p. 855.

19. Guido De Ruggiero, *The History of European Liberalism*, trans. R. G. Collingwood (Boston: Beacon Press, 1959), pp. 128–29.

20. De Ruggiero, *European Liberalism*, pp. 93 and 128.

21. Murray, vol. 6, p. 238.

22. In 1847 Cockburn wrote: "I have scarcely been able to detect any Candidate's address which, if professing Conservatism, does not explain that this means 'Liberal Conservatism.'" Cited in Murray, vol. 6, p. 238.

23. In this section I am indebted to the argument developed in Ruggiero, *European Liberalism*, pp. 94–123.

24. De Ruggiero, *European Liberalism*, p. 99.

25. Ibid., p. 102.

26. Ibid., p. 106.

27. John D. Rosenberg, *The Darkening Glass: A Portrait of Ruskin's Genius* (New York: Columbia University Press, 1961), p. 131.

28. John Ruskin, *Unto This Last* (New York: John Wiley and Sons, 1875), p. 126.

29. De Ruggiero, *European Liberalism*, p. 109.

30. Ibid., p. 110.

31. Ibid., pp. 111–12.

32. Joseph Dorfman, *The Economic Mind in American Civilization*, vol. 3 (New York: Viking Press, 1949), pp. 142, 146.

33. De Ruggiero, *European Liberalism*, p. 116.

34. John Dewey, "A Liberal Speaks Out for Liberalism," *New York Times*, February 23, 1936, sect. 7, p. 3.

35. De Ruggiero, *European Liberalism*, pp. 133–35. Cf. Lochner v. New York, 198 U.S. 45 (1905).

36. Neill, *Rise and Decline*, p. 228.

37. Max Lerner, *It's Later Than You Think: The Need for a Militant Democracy* (New York: Viking Press, 1939), p. 9.

38. De Ruggiero, *European Liberalism*, p. 140.

39. Neill, *Rise and Decline*, pp. 234–35.

40. Neill, "Liberalism," p. 342.

41. De Ruggiero, *European Liberalism*, p. 142.

42. Ibid.

43. Neill, *Rise and Decline*, p. 245.

44. John S. Mill, "A Crisis in My Mental History: One Stage Onward," in *Victorian Prose*, ed. Frederick Roe (New York: Ronald Press, 1947), pp. 218–35. See, generally, Maurice Cowling, *Mill and Liberalism* (Cambridge, Eng.: Cambridge University Press, 1963).

45. Quoted in Neill, *Rise and Decline*, p. 228. This statement does not appear in the original 1848 edition of Mill's *Principles of Political Economy*, but it does appear in all editions subsequent to 1852.

46. Quoted in Neill, *Rise and Decline*, pp. 10–11.

47. De Ruggiero, *European Liberalism*, p. 149.

48. Neill, "Liberalism," pp. 342–43.

49. Thomas D. Ungs, "Liberal-Conservative: The Sense and Nonsense of Political Labels," *University of Wichita Bulletin* (February 1964):10.

50. Samuel H. Beer, "Liberalism and the National Idea," *Left, Right, and Center: Essays on Liberalism and Conservatism in the United States*, ed. Robert A. Goldwin (Chicago: Rand McNally & Company, 1965), p. 147.

51. Quoted in Neill, *Rise and Decline*, p. 284.

52. Quoted in De Ruggiero, *European Liberalism*, p. 151.

53. Quoted in Neill, *Rise and Decline*, p. 291.

54. Fyfe, *British Liberal Party*.

55. John Maynard Keynes, *Essays in Persuasion* (New York: Harcourt, Brace & Co., 1932), pp. 323–24.

56. Ibid., p. 325.

57. Ibid., p. 335.

58. Ibid., pp. 335, 327, 345.

3. The United States Background until 1932

1. Giovanni Sartori, *Democratic Theory* (New York: Frederick A. Praeger, Inc., 1965), p. 358.

2. Quoted in Samuel H. Beer, "Liberalism and the National Idea," *Left, Right, and Center: Essays on Liberalism and Conservatism in the United States*, ed. Robert A. Goldwin (Chicago: Rand McNally & Company, 1965), p. 144. See also Ronald D. Rotunda, John E. Nowak, and J. Nelson Young, *Treatise on Constitutional Law: Substance and Procedure*, vol. 3 (St. Paul: West Publishing Co., 1985), sects. 23.19–23.23.

3. Ibid.

4. Earle Dudley Ross, *The Liberal Republican Movement* (New York: Henry Holt and Company, 1919), p. 28.

5. See, generally, Norma Peterson, *Freedom and Franchise: The Political Career of B. Gratz Brown* (Columbia, Mo.: University of Missouri Press, 1965), pp. 174–90.

6. Ross, *Liberal Republican Movement*, p. 28.

7. Thomas S. Barclay, *The Liberal Republican Movement in Missouri: 1865–1871* (Columbia, Mo.: State Historical Society of Missouri, 1926), pp. 272–73.

8. Ross, *Liberal Republican Movement*, pp. 30–31.

9. Ibid., p. 25.

10. Ibid., pp. 24–25.

11. Dumas Malone, ed., *Dictionary of American Biography*, vol. 16 (New York: Charles Scribner's Sons, 1935), p. 466; Ross, *Liberal Republican Movement*, p. 5.

12. Ross, *Liberal Republican Movement*, p. 14.

13. Ibid., pp. 30–31.

14. *New York Times*, October 31, 1872, p. 6; November 1, 1872, p. 4; November 2, 1872, p. 6; November 4, 1872, p. 4; November 5, 1872, p. 4.

15. Peterson, *Freedom and Franchise*, p. 198.

16. Richard Allen Gerber, "The Liberal Republican Alliance of 1872" (Ph.D. diss., University of Michigan, 1967), p. 7.

17. *New York Times*, November 4, 1872, p. 4.

18. Ross, *Liberal Republican Movement*, p. 16.

19. T. H. Williams, Richard N. Current, and Frank Freidel, *A History of the United States Since 1865* (New York: Alfred A. Knopf, 1961), p. 105.

20. Ibid., pp. 105–106.

21. Ibid., p. 106.

22. Allen Johnson and Dumas Malone, eds., *Dictionary of American Biography*, vol. 3 (New York: Charles Scribner's Sons, 1931), p. 533.

23. Williams, Current, and Freidel, *A History*, p. 106. For an example of the political abuse leveled at Horace Greeley see Everett Chamberlin, *The Struggle of '72* (Chicago: Union Publishing Company, 1872), chap. 25.

24. Williams, Current, and Freidel, *A History*, p. 107.

25. Charles Forcey, *The Crossroads of Liberalism* (New York: Oxford University Press, 1961), p. viii; Arthur S. Link, *Woodrow Wilson and the Progressive Era* (New York: Harper & Brothers, 1954), pp. 18–20.

26. Quoted in ibid., p. 153.

27. Henry F. Pringle, *Theodore Roosevelt* (New York: Harcourt, Brace & Co., 1931), p. 575.

28. Forcey, *Crossroads*, pp. 152–55.

29. Charles Forcey, "Intellectuals in Crisis: Croly, Weyl, Lippmann, and the 'New Republic': 1900–1919" (Ph.D. diss., University of Wisconsin, 1954), p. 510.

30. Link, *Woodrow Wilson*, p. 237. See also Mark DeWolfe Howe, ed., *The Holmes-Laski Letters*, vol. 1 (Cambridge, Mass.: Harvard University Press, 1953), pp. 16 and 33.

31. Forcey, "Intellectuals," p. 522.

32. Ibid., p. 523.

33. Ibid., p. 515.

34. Ibid., pp. 523–28. See also Link, *Woodrow Wilson*, pp. 240–41.

35. Forcey, "Intellectuals," pp. 527–28, *n*16.

36. Forcey, *Crossroads*, p. 255.

37. Towne v. Eisner, 245 U.S. 418, 425 (1918) (Holmes, J.).

38. Alan P. Grimes, "The Pragmatic Course of Liberalism," *Western Political Quarterly* 9 (September 1956):637.

39. Beer, "Liberalism," p. 147.

40. June 6, 1921, p. 7.

41. September 7, 1922, p. 19; November 6, 1922, p. 2.

42. November 6, 1922, p. 2.

43. June 23, 1923, p. 11.

44. December 8, 1924, p. 17.

45. *New York Times*, February 17, 1927, p. 20.

46. *New York Times*, August 18, 1919, p. 7.

47. See, generally, Belle Case LaFollette and Fola LaFollette, *Robert M. LaFollette* (New York: Macmillan Co., 1953), pp. 996–1014.

48. *New York Times*, July 17, 1920, p. 2.

49. *New York Times*, July 20, 1920, p. 1.

50. *New York Times*, July 17, 1920, p. 2.

51. Fred Greenbaum, *Robert Marion LaFollette* (Boston: Twayne Publishers, 1975), pp. 211–19.

52. *New York Times*, February 5, 1920, p. 7.

53. Samuel H. Church, *The Liberal Party in America: Its Principles and Its Platform* (New York: G. P. Putnam's Sons, 1931), pp. 4–5.

54. *New York Times*, February 10, 1930, p. 11.

55. February 10, 1930, p. 11.

56. Thomas P. Neill, "Liberalism . . . A Term of Many Meanings Whose Sense Must be Defined When Used," *Social Order* (October 1954):344.

57. *New York Times*, September 22, 1919, p. 7.

58. *New York Times*, September 14, 1919, sect. 3, p. 1; August 30, 1922, sect. 2, p. 4.

59. *New York Times*, February 10, 1930, p. 11.

60. *New York Times*, February 5, 1940, p. 17; April 23, 1930, p. 1.

61. Church, *Liberal Party*, p. 3.

62. Ibid., p. 21.

63. R. G. Tugwell, "The New Deal: The Progressive Tradition," *Western Political Quarterly* 3 (September 1950):400; see also James A. Wechsler, *The Age of Suspicion* (New York: Random House, 1953), p. 45.

64. *New York Times*, November 10, 1923, p. 5. See also Nicholas Murray Butler, *The Faith of a Liberal* (New York: Charles Scribner's Sons, 1924), pp. 6, 14; quoted from an address delivered before the Round Table Club, St. Louis, November 9, 1923.

65. *New York Times*, November 10, 1923, p. 5. See also Butler, *Faith of a Liberal*, pp. 11–14.

66. *New York Times*, September 18, 1925, p. 6.

67. *New York Times*, September 21, 1923, p. 4.

68. Arthur M. Schlesinger, Jr., *The Age of Roosevelt*, vol. 1 (Boston: Houghton Mifflin Company, 1957), pp. 40–41.

69. *New York Times*, September 18, 1925, p. 6.

70. Ibid.

71. *New York Times*, July 24, 1926, p. 1.

72. *New York Times*, November 23, 1929, p. 23.

73. April 28, 1922, p. 16.

74. August 8, 1923, sect. 2, p. 6.

75. November 25, 1931, p. 20.

76. September 28, 1924, sect. 2, p. 4.

77. February 6, 1930, p. 22.

78. Quoted in Beer, "Liberalism," p. 148, n7. See also B. F. Wright, Jr., *A Sourcebook of American Political Theory* (New York: Macmillan Co., 1929), p. 639.

79. "Text of President Hoover's Address: Kings Mountain Battlefield, S.C.," *New York Times*, October 8, 1930, p. 18.

80. "Hoover in Warning on Red Doctrines," *New York Times*, October 8, 1930, pp. 1, 18.

4. The Great Debate: 1932–1940

1. Frank Freidel, *Franklin D. Roosevelt: The Ordeal* (Boston: Little, Brown & Co., 1954), p. 57; T. H. Williams, Richard Current, and Frank Freidel, *A History of the United States Since 1865* (New York: Alfred A. Knopf, 1961), p. 322.

2. Arthur Schlesinger, Jr., *The Age of Roosevelt*, vol. 1 (Boston: Houghton Mifflin Company, 1957), pp. 80, 81; David Burner, *Herbert Hoover: A Public Life* (New York: Alfred A. Knopf, 1979), pp. 153–54.

3. Freidel, *Franklin D. Roosevelt*, p. 57. See also Edgar Robinson and Vaughn Bornet, *Herbert Hoover, President of the United States* (Stanford, Ca.: Hoover Institution Press, 1975), p. 12.

4. Schlesinger, *Age of Roosevelt*, vol. 1, pp. 84–87; Williams, Current, and Freidel, *A History*, pp. 408–409.

5. Finis Farr, *F.D.R.* (New Rochelle, N.Y.: Arlington House, 1972), pp. 167–68.

6. Quoted in Williams, Current, and Freidel, *A History*, p. 408.

7. Williams, Current, and Freidel, *A History*, p. 377; Warren Sloat, *1929: America Before the Crash* (New York: Macmillan Co., 1979), pp. 220–21.

8. Williams, Current, and Freidel, *A History*, p. 430; Burner, *Herbert Hoover*, p. 174.

9. Williams, Current, and Freidel, *A History*, p. 440; Freidel, *Franklin D. Roosevelt*, pp. 417–18.

10. Rexford G. Tugwell, "The Protagonists: Roosevelt and Hoover," *Antioch Review* 13 (December 1953):419.

11. Thomas H. Greer, *What Roosevelt Thought* (East Lansing, Mich.: Michigan State University Press, 1958), p. 52.

12. Quoted in Schlesinger, *Age of Roosevelt*, vol. 1, p. 290. See also Arthur A. Eirch, Jr., *Ideologies and Utopias: The Impact of the New Deal on American Thought* (Chicago: Quadrangle Books, 1969), pp. 81–82.

13. Frank Freidel and Norman Pollack, eds., *Builders of American Institutions* (Chicago: Rand McNally, 1963), pp. 457–58.

14. Elliot A. Rosen, *Hoover, Roosevelt, and the Brain Trust* (New York: Columbia University Press, 1977), pp. 297–301.

15. Tugwell, "The Protagonists," p. 442.

16. R. G. Tugwell, "The New Deal: The Progressive Tradition," *Western Political Quarterly* 3 (September 1950):396–97.

17. See Louis Hartz, *The Liberal Tradition in America* (New York: Harcourt, Brace & World, Inc., 1955). Hartz uses the term "liberal" in a very specific manner: the philosophy of John Locke. Compare with Jay Sigler, *The Conservative Tradition in American Thought* (New York: Putnam, 1969).

18. Hartz, *The Liberal Tradition*, p. 262

19. Tugwell, "The New Deal," p. 400; Thurmond W. Arnold, *The Symbols of Government* (New Haven: Yale University Press, 1935), pp. 238–89. See also Ronald D. Rotunda, John E. Nowak, and J. Nelson Young, *Treatise on Constitutional Law: Substance and Procedure*, vol. 2 (St. Paul: West Publishing Co., 1985), sect. 15.3.

20. Arnold, *Symbols*, pp. 252–53, 232.

21. Edgar E. Robinson, *They Voted for Roosevelt* (Stanford, Ca.: Stanford University Press, 1947), p. 4.

22. Samuel I. Rosenman, *Working with Roosevelt* (New York: Harper & Brothers, 1952), pp. 41–42.

23. Franklin D. Roosevelt, *The Public Papers and Addresses of Franklin D. Roosevelt*, vol. 7, ed. Samuel Rosenman (New York: Macmillan Co., 1941), p. xxxi.

24. Samuel H. Beer, "Liberalism and the National Idea," *Left, Right, and Center: Essays on Liberalism and Conservatism in the United States*, ed. Robert A. Goldwin (Chicago: Rand McNally & Company, 1965), p. 146.

25. William E. Leuchtenburg, *Franklin D. Roosevelt and the New Deal, 1932–1940* (New York: Harper and Row, Publishers, 1963), p. 8; Schlesinger, *Age of Roosevelt*, vol. 1, pp. 523–25, *n*30.

26. Personal communication, November 22, 1966.

27. Tugwell, "The New Deal," pp. 391–92.

28. Personal communication, November 22, 1966.

29. Personal communication, October 26, 1966.

30. Quoted in Freidel, *Franklin D. Roosevelt*, pp. 54, 282, n6.

31. See Schlesinger, *Age of Roosevelt*, vol. 1, pp. 277, 520–21, n5.

32. Personal communication, October 26, 1966.

33. Daniel Fusfeld, *The Economic Thought of Franklin D. Roosevelt and the Origins of the New Deal* (New York: Columbia University Press, 1954), pp. 226–27.

34. Quoted in Greer, *What Roosevelt Thought*, p. 211.

35. Leuchtenburg, *Franklin D. Roosevelt*, p. 35.

36. Hartz, *The Liberal Tradition*, p. 262.

37. Greer, *What Roosevelt Thought*, p. 54.

38. Tugwell, "The New Deal," pp. 400–401.

39. Quoted in Beer, "Liberalism," p. 147. See also Schlesinger, *Age of Roosevelt*, vol. 1, p. 313.

40. Personal communication, October 26, 1966.

41. Quoted in Leuchtenburg, *Franklin D. Roosevelt*, p. 45.

42. "The Excitement of the Hundred Days," in *The New Deal and the American People*, ed. Frank Freidel (Englewood Cliffs, N.J.: Prentice-Hall, Inc., 1964), p. 5.

43. Ibid., p. 8.

44. Arthur M. Schlesinger, Jr., *The Age of Roosevelt*, vol. 2 (Boston: Houghton Mifflin Co., 1958), p. 22.

45. Quoted in *New York Times*, July 16, 1933, sect. 4, p. 4.

46. *New York Times*, December 7, 1933, p. 22.

47. *Texaco Star*, March–April, 1933, p. 4.

48. See Schlesinger, *Age of Roosevelt*, vol. 2, p. 471.

49. Ibid., p. 486; V. O. Key, Jr., *Politics, Parties, and Pressure Groups* (New York: Thomas Y. Crowell Company, 1964), p. 189; Denis W. Brogan, *The Era of Franklin D. Roosevelt* (New Haven: Yale University Press, 1950), pp. 197–98.

50. Burner, *Herbert Hoover*, pp. 329–30.

51. Schlesinger, *Age of Roosevelt*, vol. 2, pp. 487–88.

52. Ibid., p. 472.

53. Herbert Hoover, *The Challenge to Liberty* (New York: Charles Scribner's Sons, 1934), pp. 4, 7–8, 60–61.

54. *New York Times*, October 18, 1934, p. 22.

55. Ibid., October 22, 1934, p. 14.

56. Ibid., October 25, 1934, p. 22.

57. Ibid., December 29, 1934, p. 6.

58. Ibid., October 1, 1934, p. 16.

59. Beer, "Liberalism," p. 148.

60. P. W. Wilson, "Liberalism Faces a World Challenge," *New York Times Magazine*, March 11, 1934, pp. 10, 20.

61. *New York Times*, October 1, 1934, p. 3.

62. Schlesinger, *Age of Roosevelt*, vol. 2, p. 489.

63. Williams, Current, and Freidel, *A History*, p. 500. One of the Senate seats was filled by Harry S. Truman.

64. Tugwell, "The New Deal," p. 390.

65. Williams, Current, and Freidel, *A History*, pp. 500, 502.

66. Raymond Moley, with the assistance of Elliot A. Rosen, *The First New Deal* (New York: Harcourt, Brace & World, Inc., 1966), p. 526.

67. Tugwell, "The New Deal," pp. 399–400.

68. *New York Times*, January 6, 1935, sect. 4, p. 1.

69. Ibid.

70. Key, *Politics*, p. 189; Robinson, *They Voted for Roosevelt*, p. 33.

71. Brogan, *Era*, p. 199. See also Robinson, *They Voted for Roosevelt*, p. 33.

72. *New York Times*, April 19, 1936, p. 28.

73. Ibid., March 8, 1936, pp. 1, 36.

74. See Rosenman, *Working with Roosevelt*, p. 110.

75. John Dewey, "A Liberal Speaks Out for Liberalism," *New York Times Magazine*, February 3, 1936, pp. 3, 24.

76. *New York Times*, October 18, 1936, sect. 4, p. 8.

77. Ibid., March 2, 1936, p. 16.

78. Ibid., June 8, 1936, p. 14.

79. Key, *Politics*, pp. 189–90.

80. Moley, *The First New Deal*, p. 527. Arthur Krock writes that he agrees with Moley's explanation; personal communication, December 7, 1966.

81. Frank Latham, *FDR and the Supreme Court Fight, 1937: A President Tries to Reorganize the Federal Judiciary* (New York: Franklin Watts, Inc., 1972), p. 4; Robert G. McCloskey, *The American Supreme Court* (Chicago: University of Chicago Press, 1960), p. 169.

82. Alpheus T. Mason and William M. Beaney, *American Constitutional Law* (Englewood Cliffs, N.J.: Prentice-Hall, Inc., 1964), p. 221. See, generally, John E. Nowak, Ronald D. Rotunda, and J. Nelson Young, *Constitutional Law* (St. Paul: West Publishing Co., 1978), pp. 38–39, 146–50.

83. Mason and Beaney, *American Constitutional Law*, p. 222. See also Ronald D. Rotunda, *Modern Constitutional Law* (St. Paul: West Publishing Co., 1981), pp. 206–207.

84. Justice Roberts, in particular, appeared to leave the conservative bloc and join the liberal bloc. It was said that he was "the switch in time that saved nine." In fact Roberts privately announced his vote in one case—West Coast Hotel v. Parrish, 300 U.S. 379 (1937), upholding a state minimum wage law in a 5 to 4 vote—*before* the Court-packing plan

was unveiled, but *after* the November election returns. See Rotunda, *Modern Constitutional Law*, p. 207.

85. Mason and Beaney, *American Constitutional Law*, p. 223.

86. *New York Times*, June 10, 1937, p. 18.

87. Ibid., October 23, 1937, p. 16.

88. Ibid., October 26, 1937, p. 22; October 27, 1937, p. 30; October 31, 1937, sect. 4, p. 9.

89. Ibid., October 26, 1937, p. 22; October 27, 1937, p. 30.

90. Greer, *What Roosevelt Thought*, p. 119; Leuchtenburg, *Franklin D. Roosevelt*, p. 266.

91. Leuchtenburg, *Franklin D. Roosevelt*, p. 267; *New York Times*, June 25, 1938, pp. 1, 3.

92. *New York Times*, September 3, 1938, p. 1.

93. Quoted in *New York Times*, June 26, 1938, p. 2. See also Ellis W. Hawley, *The New Deal and the Problem of Monopoly* (Princeton, N.J.: Princeton University Press, 1966), p. 424.

94. Leuchtenburg, *Franklin D. Roosevelt*, p. 259.

95. Ibid., p. 269.

96. Franklin D. Roosevelt, *Public Papers*, vol. 7, pp. xxxi–xxxii.

97. Greer, *What Roosevelt Thought*, pp. 119–120; Arthur M. Schlesinger, Jr., *History of U.S. Political Parties*, 4 vols. (New York: Chelsea House Publishers, 1973), 3:1950. Representative John O'Connor, House Rules Committee chairman, was defeated but "mostly for local reasons."

98. Williams, Current, and Freidel, *A History*, pp. 513, 515–16, 520.

99. Leuchtenburg, *Franklin D. Roosevelt*, p. 269, n50.

100. Ibid., p. 268.

101. *New York Times*, November 7, 1938, p. 9; *New York Times*, September 4, 1938, p. 2.

102. Ibid., September 25, 1938, p. 3; July 11, 1938, p. 4; September 25, 1938, sect. 4, p. 9; July 3, 1938, sect. 4, p. 9.

103. *Des Moines Register* editorial, quoted in *New York Times*, June 26, 1938, p. 2; *New York Times*, July 1, 1938, p. 9; September 28, 1938, p. 6.

104. For example, during 1938 and 1939, definitions of "conservative" began to appear in the *New York Times*: July 11, 1938, p. 4; September 6, 1938, p. 1, 3, and editorial p. 20; September 8, 1938, p. 22; September 25, 1938, p. 3; July 6, 1939, p. 2; July 9, 1952, p. 5; July 14, 1939, p. 18; July 16, 1939, sect. 4, p. 9; July 23, 1939, sect. 4, p. 9.

105. Williams, Current, and Freidel, *A History*, p. 520.

106. *New York Times*, August 12, 1939, p. 1; Williams, Current, and Freidel, *A History*, p. 541.

107. *New York Times*, July 9, 1939, p. 5.

5. Roosevelt and a National Liberal Party

1. For example, see Thomas H. Greer, *What Roosevelt Thought* (East Lansing, Mich.: Michigan State University Press, 1958), pp. 123–24; Ernest K. Lindley, *The Roosevelt Revolution* (New York: Viking Press, 1933), pp. 10–11.

2. Greer, *What Roosevelt Thought*, p. 120.

3. Samuel I. Rosenman, *Working with Roosevelt* (New York: Harper & Brothers, 1952), p. 464. Much of the remainder of this section is based on Rosenman, chap. 24, pp. 463–70. See also James MacGregor Burns, *Roosevelt: The Soldier of Freedom* (New York: Harcourt Brace Jovanovich, Inc., 1970), pp. 511–12.

4. I am indebted to Professor Frank Freidel, who holds this opinion and who first suggested to me this argument.

5. Frank Freidel, *America in the Twentieth Century* (New York: Alfred A. Knopf, 1960), p. 448.

6. Rosenman, *Working with Roosevelt*, p. 466.

7. *F.D.R.: His Personal Letters, 1928–45*, vol. 2, ed. Elliott Roosevelt (New York: Duell, Sloan and Pearce, 1950), p. 1520. Roosevelt had assured Willkie that the meeting would be off the record.

8. Rosenman, *Working with Roosevelt*, p. 466.

9. Ibid.

10. The July 13 letter was published almost verbatim in the *New York Times* of August 12, 1944.

11. Denis W. Brogan, *The Era of Franklin D. Roosevelt* (New Haven: Yale University Press, 1950), pp. 352–53.

12. Freidel, *America*, p. 449.

13. Brogan, *Era of Roosevelt*, p. 353.

6. The Epilogue to the Great Debate

1. Information about this poll is taken from Thomas P. Neill, *The Rise and Decline of Liberalism* (Milwaukee: Bruce Publishing Company, 1953), pp. 3–4, and Robert Bendiner, "Politics and People," *Nation* 168 (March 26, 1949):349–50.

2. Clinton Rossiter, *Conservatism in America* (New York: 1962), p. 195; James W. Prothro, "Verbal Shifts in the American Presidency: A Content Analysis," *American Political Science Review* 50 (September 1956):727.

3. *New York Times*, June 28, 1963, p. 33.

4. David McCord Wright, "When You Call Me Conservative, Smile," *Fortune* 43:2 (May 1951):76–77, 192.

5. Robert A. Taft, "What Is a Liberal?" *Commercial and Financial Chronicle* 163:2 (May 16, 1946):2668.

6. Louis Bromfield, "The Triumph of the Egghead," *Freeman* 3 (December 1, 1952):157.

7. Leon Shull, executive director, ADA, quoted in *New York Times*, June 15, 1980, p. 14.

8. *New York Times*, June 30, 1980, p. 19.

9. Ibid., October 6, 1981, p. 26.

10. Ibid., January 22, 1978, p. 1.

11. Ibid., p. 30.

12. Ibid.

13. Ibid.

14. Ibid., September 20, 1980, p. 19.

15. Arthur Schlesinger, Jr., "Is Liberalism Dead?" *New York Times*, March 30, 1980, pp. 42, 73.

16. *Wall Street Journal*, March 6, 1985, p. 60; *New York Times*, October 6, 1981, p. 26; *Wall Street Journal*, March 8, 1985, p. 48.

17. *Wall Street Journal*, March 6, 1985, p. 60.

18. Thurmond Arnold, *The Symbols of Government* (New Haven: Yale University Press, 1935), pp. 258–59.

19. Ibid.

20. Quoted in C. K. Ogden and I. A. Richards, *The Meaning of Meaning* (New York: Harcourt, Brace & Co., 1923), p. xxiv. See James Boyd White, *When Words Lose Their Meaning: Constitutions and Reconstitutions of Language, Character, and Community* (Chicago: University of Chicago Press, 1984), pp. 275–76.

21. Neill, *Rise and Decline*, p. 6. See also A. James Gregor, *An Introduction to Metapolitics* (New York: Free Press, 1971), p. 77: "Language is at once a commonplace and a great puzzlement. It is the principal vehicle of communication . . . and yet it is a treacherous source of confusion."

Afterword

1. (Oxford: Oxford University Press, 1961). See also N. MacCormick, *H. L. A. Hart* (London: Clarendon Press, 1981). Also influential in this regard are the works of one of Hart's former students, Joseph Raz; see *The Concept of a Legal System* (Oxford: Oxford University Press, 1970) and *The Authority of Law* (Oxford: Oxford University Press, 1979).

2. Eds. P. Hacker and J. Raz (Oxford: Oxford University Press, 1979).

3. The Critical Legal Studies Movement founded in the 1970s by

scholars such as Mark Kelman, Duncan Kennedy, and Morton Horwitz is now beginning to have a major impact on legal scholarship, though not yet to the extent of the "law and economics" movement. See, for instance, R. M. Unger, *The Critical Legal Studies Movement*, 96 HARV. L. REV. 563 (1983), and Note, *Round and Round the Bramble Bush: From Legal Realism to Critical Legal Scholarship*, 95 HARV. L. REV. 1669 (1982). The first collection of CLS essays has been recently published in D. Kairys, ed., *The Politics of Law: A Progressive Critique* (New York: Pantheon Books, 1982); see the review by Sanford Levinson, *Escaping Liberalism: Easier Said than Done*, 96 HARV. L. REV. 1466 (1983).

4. See J. Austin, *The Province of Jurisprudence Determined*, 2d ed. (London: Weidenfeld & Nicholson, 1954). See also the treatment of the Austinian sanction theory in Hart, *The Concept of Law*, p. 18. On Austin in general, see W. L. Morison, *John Austin* (Stanford, Ca.: Stanford University Press, 1982).

5. See Hart, *The Concept of Law*, p. 16.

6. Ibid., p. 112.

7. Ibid., pp. 55–56, 84.

8. Ibid., pp. 84–85.

9. Ibid., pp. 111–13.

10. Hart, *The Concept of Law*, p. 85.

11. Ibid., p. 181.

12. Ibid., p. 77.

13. Hacker and Raz, *Law, Morality, and Society*.

14. R. S. Summers, "Naive Instrumentalism and the Law," in *Law, Morality, and Society*, eds. P. Hacker and J. Raz, p. 119.

15. See especially M. Horwitz, *The Transformation of American Law 1780–1860* (Cambridge, Mass.: Harvard University Press, 1977), building, in part, on the insights of K. Llewellyn, *The Common Law Tradition—Deciding Appeals* (Boston: Little, Brown & Co., 1960). See also M. Tushnet, *The American Law of Slavery 1810–1860* (Chapel Hill, N.C.: University of North Carolina Press, 1981), and J. W. Hurst, *Law and Markets in United States History* (Princeton, N.J.: Princeton University Press, 1982).

16. See, for instance, the remarks of Professor Tony Freyer in T. Freyer, *Forums of Order: The Federal Courts and Business in American History* (Baltimore: Johns Hopkins University Press, 1979).

17. "Naive Instrumentalism," p. 118.

18. See Austin, *Province of Jurisprudence*; see also Summers, "Naive Instrumentalism," p. 131.

19. On the relationship between enforcement costs and the size of so-

ciety, see R. Posner, *The Economics of Justice* (Cambridge, Mass.: Harvard University Press, 1982).

20. Cf. Tushnet, *Law of Slavery*, and the criticism of it by W. A. J. Watson, *Slave Law: History and Ideology*, 91 YALE L.J. 1034 (1982).

21. Ibid., pp. 111–13.

22. Ibid., p. 77.

23. Ibid., pp. 92–94.

24. Posner, *Justice*; M. Hoeflich, "Of Reason, Gamesmanship & Taxes," 2 AM. J. TAX POLICY 1 (1983).

25. Llewellyn, *Common Law Tradition*.

26. See, for example, G. E. White, *Tort Law in America: An Intellectual History* (New York: Oxford University Press, 1980).

27. See Hoeflich, "Of Reason."

28. See, for example, D. Graber, *Verbal Behavior and Politics* (Urbana: University of Illinois Press, 1976).

Index